Organizational Design in Business

Organizational Design in Business

A New Alternative for a Complex World

Carrie Foster

BEP BUSINESS EXPERT PRESS

Organizational Design in Business: A New Alternative for a Complex World
Copyright © Business Expert Press, LLC, 2018.

First published in 2018 by
Business Expert Press, LLC
222 East 46th Street, New York, NY 10017
www.businessexpertpress.com

ISBN-13: 978-1-63157-770-3 (paperback)
ISBN-13: 978-1-63157-771-0 (e-book)

Business Expert Press Human Resource Management and Organizational Behavior Collection

Collection ISSN: 1946-5637 (print)
Collection ISSN: 1946-5645 (electronic)

Cover and interior design by S4Carlisle Publishing Services Private Ltd., Chennai, India

First edition: 2018

10 9 8 7 6 5 4 3 2 1

Printed in the United States of America.

Abstract

This book offers an alternative to the industrial revolutionary paradigm of organization that we still live and work with today and instead argues that the environmental and economic complexity of the digital age require an evolutionary leap in the purpose, design, and traits of organization. *Organizational Design in Business* tackles the subject of organization development and design through an organic and purpose-driven approach and provides practical how-to tools for managers and leaders.

This book challenges the idea that business as usual is a viable option in the digital economy. If performance is to be driven at an organizational level, and is to be sustainable, then business leaders and development professionals need to have a deep understanding of how to achieve balance in their organization in response to the complexity of the external business environment.

Keywords

Creative adaptation, leadership, organization development, organization design, organizational balance, purpose, talent management

Contents

Preface

It is the harmony of the diverse parts, their symmetry, their happy balance; in a word it is all that introduces order, all that gives unity, that permits us to see clearly and to comprehend at once both the ensemble and the details.

—Henri Poincare

Whether you are a regular consumer of books, articles, podcasts, vlogs, or ezines, when it comes to the subject of developing and improving the performance of an organization or developing people to release their talent potential, the focus will, generally, be on a single element of an organization's development: Strategy, Leadership, Management, Organizational Design, Talent Management, Lean Management, Change Management, etc.

The segregation of each part of an organization into a specialist school of thought is hardly surprising, given the complexity of organization development and the richness of thinking from academics and business practitioners all of whom subscribe to various schools of thought. Take strategy, Amazon has over 120,000 plus books on that subject, a web search on strategy development returns 784 million results, even if you allow for people using some of the same models the single subject of making an action plan for the business is vast. Models and theoretical frameworks are used by academics and practitioners alike to help break down the variables and explain the phenomenon in a way which makes it easy to understand, digest, and apply learning.

Therefore, the segregation of elements of organizational performance into a school or specialism is not necessarily a bad thing since it allows for an in-depth and informed study. The issue of course is that organizational variables don't operate in isolation but rather feed into and receive from the organizational system as a whole. Trying to understand organizational strategy outside of the organizational system is limiting from the point of view of being able to design a plan, which balances organizational performance as a whole.

Organization Design

For over 30 years, the field of organization design has been dominated by Galbraith's STAR model, (see Figure A), which offers a technostructural approach to organization design decision making. Galbraith and Kates (2007) state that, "a strategy implies a set of capabilities at which an organization must excel in order to achieve the strategic goals. There is a responsibility to design and influence the structure, processes, rewards and people practices of the organization in order to build these needed capabilities."

The STAR model seeks to improve organizational effectiveness through a focus on the organization's technology and structure. The elements of the framework are as follows:

- *Strategy.* Provides common direction, criteria for decision making, and governance structures.
- *Capabilities.* The competitive advantage provides by the set of skills, technologies, and human abilities within the organization.
- *Structure.* Aligns the structure of the organization in regard to power and authority, information flows, and organizational roles to mobilize resources to deliver effective execution of strategy.

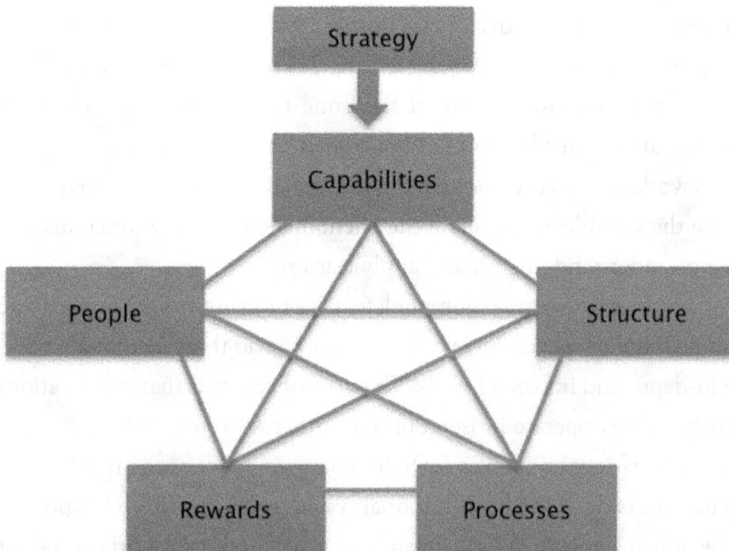

Figure A Galbraith and Kates (2007) STAR model

- *Processes and Lateral capabilities.* Aligns activity to support collaboration across boundaries, speed up decision making, and improve information sharing in order to leverage best practices.
- *Reward systems.* Ensure that the metrics and measures used to reward performance deliver the right result, increase standards, and support retention of staff.
- *People Practices.* Developing methods for deploying people into new roles, managing performance, and supporting people development to execute strategy.

The STAR model is an intelligent logical design process to ensure all the technostructural elements of organizational design are in place. It is also a deficit-based approach, which focuses on task methods, job design, division of labor, and hierarchical structure to solve problems with organizational processes. It seeks to use structure and processes to drive behavior and actions in the deployment of the strategy. Tools that can be employed include restructuring the organization, developing organization systems, business process re-engineering, and competency-based management. At the center is the alignment of efficient processes and procedures and effective execution of strategic plans.

The STAR model is a product of its time, focusing on the structure and technology of an organization in order to that the organization becomes more efficient and effective. But this approach is also the heart of the framework's weakness. Although there is a recognition of the people element within the framework, in terms of the proficient use of the human capital resource within the organization, it ignores the intangible asset of human potential in favor of a "mechanistic Victorian paradigm birthed in industrialization . . . focused on processes and efficiency saving" (Foster, 2017a). Galbraith and Kates (2007) argue that, "Although culture is an essential part of an organization, it is not an explicit part of the model because the leader cannot design the culture directly. An organization's culture consists of the common values, mindsets, and norms of behavior that have emerged over time and that most employees share. It is an outcome of the cumulative design decisions that have been made in the past and of the leadership and management behaviors that result from those decisions." But it is, as many organizations will attest, culture that destroys change management efforts if the human element of organizational life is ignored in the organization design process. It is the social construct of the organization that is formed out of the values, mindsets, and norms of behavior of individual employees within an organization that will determine whether the mechanical design of the organization will function or be dysfunctional.

This book seeks to address this gap. The STAR framework of organization design and lean methodologies contribute to designing the technostructural elements of an organization. Scientific management approaches were preeminent in industrialized nations during the twentieth century because production lines benefit from mechanistic approaches. However, today's global economy is based on knowledge, innovation, and creativity. Designing efficient processes works well when making goods, but struggles when an organization's competitive advantage is based on what people can create and communicate. Ignoring the people potential element is to disregard the fundamental organization design variable that produces sustainable organizational performance in the twenty-first century. Even the most well-designed process in the world will fail if the attitudes and behavior of employees mean that what they input into the process or procedure is wrong. Processes that are badly designed can still produce a high-performing world-class organization, if the people working in it have the values, mindset, and behavior that allow them to create, innovate, and perform despite the dysfunction. This same fortitude can overcome reward failures, bad organizational structure, and even lack of training. It's amazing what humans can achieve. The Holy Grail of Organization Design is well-designed processes, which free people to release their full potential. But it is the human variable that will always determine sustainable performance and the success or failure of an enterprise.

Organizations need to change because society has changed. The world we live in is different, but organizations in the digital age must progress and evolve from the prevailing Victorian industrialized paradigm. The hierarchical technostructural approaches to organization design are no longer fully fit for purpose in today's fast-moving, knowledge-intensive world. The evolution toward the internet of things means that organizations operating in the modern global economy need to adapt their traditional thinking of how they operate to a philosophy that embraces the natural cycles, systems, controls, and available talent within the organization in order to achieve balance and create an environment for sustainable performance. This is where the Organization Balance model seeks to offer an alternative approach to organization design.

Organization Balance—A People-Led Approach

From the perspective of achieving organizational balance, all the elements of an organization's performance need to operate together in the same way as an ecosystem. This approach is separate from the organizational ecology school of thinking; the proposed alternative is to find a balance in all the key areas involving people, who in this context *are* the organization, in order to create sustainable performance. It is necessary to understand the interrelationship of different people interactions within an organization that impact on organizational performance. Consideration needs to be given not just to the interplay of the organization's shareholders, customers, and competitors but also the behaviors, leadership processes, the context in which leaders and employees operate, available talent potential, how people integrate and communicate, social capital, how work is executed, and the way in which the organization interacts with other people in the external environment. Keeping with the ecosystem theme, the central tenet of Organization Balance is that performance comes from exploring a holistic and an organic rather than artificially manufactured approach to creating sustainable performance within an organization.

Acknowledgments

I am grateful to Premkumar Narayanan for his never-ending patience during the editing process. A special thanks is also owed to Scott Isenberg and the team at Business Expert Press for giving me a platform to share my ideas.

A special thanks goes out to my husband who suffered me taking my laptop on a family camping trip this summer in order to get this book finished and buying me a hat and woolly socks in August to keep me warm at night. This book was the first book I ever tried to write and had been part-written for too long while other books have germinated from idea to publication. During that time Sandra and David Foster, Margaret and Jeremy Ashton, Chris and Dave Ashton-Hollis, Sue and Ollie Poulter, Becky and Sharif Omar, and Alan and Helen Poulter have encouraged me to keep going during a personal transition where I have sought to find purposeful endeavor. Your enduring patience with my nutty pursuit for authenticity has given me safe harbor when it has felt too difficult. Finally, I must thank my children for keeping me grounded. To Lily Grace, thank you for reminding me that I don't do a real job, and my son, for complaining that I am always working. Keeping it real, always.

CHAPTER 1

Introduction

Organizational context is changing continuously. Amid a significant shift in the political climate in industrialized Western democracies, high levels of demographic changes, social, technological, and digital revolution and a shift in established patterns of globalization, organizational leaders need to design organizations to survive and navigate the environment to deliver sustainable performance. The challenge is to find balance in the maelstrom of complexity, to balance flexibility with consistency, agility with harmony, and speed with consideration.

The Importance of Balance

From an organizational balance perspective, all things are equal. Every part of an organization is part of a system that relies on and impacts other elements of the organization. For example, leadership is affected by the structure of the organization, the individuals who are leaders, the individuals they lead, the internal and the external environment, and so on. It is not possible to change one element of the organization without impacting on another and at the same time the change that is made is determined by the other elements. Like an ecosystem in the natural world, every element is "part of, a determinate of and a product of the system, and can only be sustained if kept in balance with the other organizational elements" (Foster, 2017a). Change any one part of an organization, deliberately or by accident, and the balance of an organization changes—for good or bad. What is more, the continued success or eventual failure of organizational endeavors will be determined by how much the organization works with, rather than against, human nature and the organizational ecosystem.

Work against the human organizational system and resistance, drag, and natural barriers will affect the success of an organization's performance. Work within the organizational system and the result will be performance, which is self-sustaining. If performance is to be driven at an organizational level and is to be sustainable, there needs to be a deep understanding of the balance of the organization. This means when change comes, the potential for performance comes not just from the area immediately affected, but from harnessing and transforming the energy created by the change through rebalancing the whole of the organization. It is not that an organization cannot perform without balance in its system, but it cannot perform to its full potential, and performance will not be sustainable over the long term. Like any ecosystem, change occurs both inside and outside the control of the organization. The key to continued peak organizational performance is to be open to the changes required and pro-actively adjust and make changes in order to maintain balance. In recent years, there has been a move in all sorts of areas of human activity such that of balance and harmony; organic farming, sustainable housing, and green business practices. All these developments are the result of a realization and understanding that in trying to control and impose an artificial structure while ignoring the relationship between humans and their environment results in inflicting long-term damage to our environment and is less effective than using natural resources, cycles, and controls.

Model of Organizational Balance

The same is true in an organization. Rather than fighting against the internal and external environment, trying to impose unnatural order, like the proverbial concrete jungle, an organization can find balance and create an environment for sustainable performance by embracing an organization's naturally occurring resources, cycles, and controls. Foster (2017a) introduced the model of organizational balance (Figure 1.1) to "provide a map to navigate specific elements of organizational performance from the perspective of a people-centred ecosystem."

The model of organizational balance provides a framework of interrelationships and interactions that are specific to the human processes within the organization, which have an impact upon the sustainable organizational

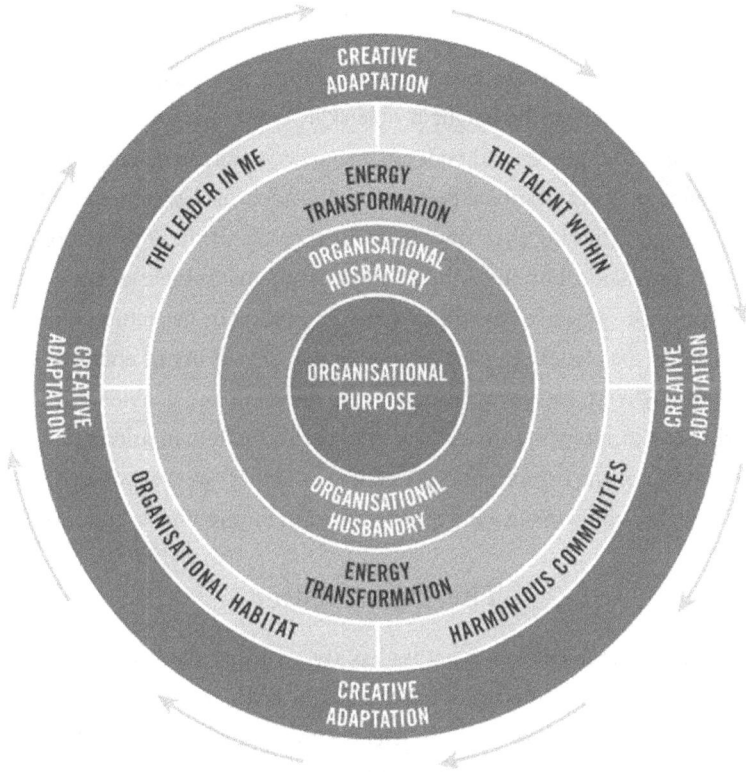

Figure 1.1 *Model of organizational balance*

performance. Taking into account the holistic nature of an organization, each section of the framework describes a human process element of the organizational ecosystem, which interacts with other elements and results in a positive or negative impact upon organizational performance.

Organizational Purpose

An organization requires a reason to exists, and its purpose gives meaning to the organizations day-to-day activities. Strategic management and planning helps the business leader focus on how to deliver an organizations strategy but fails to explain where strategy is created. In a modern global economy, the center of balance is at the heart of the organization and must answer not with what must the people in the organization must do, but with why they are here, giving meaning to an organization's day-to-day activities.

The Leader in Me

There are two types of leaders: Leaders of People and Leaders of Expertise. Just because you can be taught people skills does not mean you have the potential to lead people, and poor leadership decisions can damage individuals, team, and organizational performance. Leaders have great responsibility not only in achieving their own tasks for the sake of the organization but also in their contribution to the creation of an environment of sustainable performance. Whatever the organization, regardless of its culture, industry, or history, the leadership process ensures that the efforts of employees are coordinated with each other. Leaders give direction and enable individuals and teams to move toward the achievement of the organization's purpose. Leadership of the organization integrates the activity of the employees and provides a linchpin for creating the environment for sustainable performance.

The Talent Within

With a mismatch between what leaders say about people being their most important asset and their people practices, in order to achieve balance, an organization should tap into the talent within the organization itself and help individual employees understand the talent within themselves. Every human being has a talent in something, which means all employees contribute to the talent with the organization. The organization needs to provide an environment, which enables individuals to understand and release the talent potential they have. The organization needs to consider how to manage and create an individual's job role around the talents they possess. Talent is also an individual responsibility, with each employee tasked with developing a self-awareness of their talent and taking steps to develop their capacity to use it. Leaders must work to help integrate the needs of the individual with that of the organization in order to create an environment in which individual purpose can be attained in line with the achievement of organizational purpose.

Harmonious Communities

In a traditional organization setting, informal groups arise on the basis of social needs of the employees within the organization. These groups are influential and develop their own leadership and hierarchy.

Organizational balance requires leaders and employees to work together to create an environment, which will encourage and facilitate individuals, teams and functions to build relationships and enable employees to collaborate in order to collectively help the organization to pursue activities to achieve its purpose and strategy. By tapping into the collective talent gathered from around the networked organization, it is possible to expand outstanding performance from a limited number of individuals to release the full talent available within the organization through successfully sharing the pool of organizational expertise, knowledge, skill, and experience.

Organizational Habitat

To enable the organization to adapt effectively to change and challenge from internal and external influences, it needs to create a networked internal architecture within the organization. Its leadership and the establishment of a system of relationships between individuals and groups determine an organization's structure. Organizational balance can only be achieved if the structure and design of an organization is agile and flexible enough to successfully respond to changes in the internal and external environment while continuing to provide the stability required to manage day-to-day organizational activities.

Organizational Husbandry

The promotion of sustainable organizational processes and practices is achieved when the organization develops a methodology of approaching the organizational resources sensitively and adopts methods of working which complements this. In addition to managing the changes in its internal environment, the organization is also part of a global system and its performance environment will be impacted by the increasing interconnectivity between global economies, corporations, and society as a whole. Organizations must understand that the ultimate consequences of any decision they make are at best poorly understood and at worst catastrophic to sustainable performance.

Creative Adaptation

With a dynamic and fast-moving organizational operating environment, it is essential that organizations develop the creative capability which ensures its operations are subject to continual innovation, maintaining a favorable operating systems and achieving sustainable performance in response to the changes in the external environment. Proactive management of changes rather than responding reactively to the changes is important to maintain organizational balance.

Energy Transformation

Irrespective of the organization, it is the conversion of a number of inputs and outputs through organizational activity which is influenced by internal and external environmental resources. It is essential that the organization takes active steps to analyze how effective its activities are and evaluate the impact and outcome of the activities. Any organizational activity utilizes time and resource (energy), and it is important that the energy that is committed delivers added value and contributes to transforming the performance of the organization. Within a system, any activity will lead to disorder, given the natural order of thing. Commitment to energy transformation manages the tension between unbalancing activities, temporary disorder, and rebalancing of order. Any activity should have the impact that the drives the organization toward the achievement of its purpose and enables the organization to align energy expended with the desired outcomes.

Organizational Cycling

The external environment in which the organization carries out its operations provides constant obstacles, which can have a disruptive influence, and requires the organization to make substantive changes on a continuous basis in order to maintain forward momentum. This may be the adoption of new technology, changes in society and cultural shifts, and the introduction of new regulations. These influences combined with other unsettling forces can disrupt the balance of the organization and its ability to create an environment for sustainable performance. Major organizations are discovering that sustainable systemic thinking is not only a requirement for longevity but also a profitable business model. The requirement for sustainability is a mix of seemingly competing demands requiring resolution to strive to create balance. Represented by arrows on the model organizational cycling is part of the other elements of organizational balance, but the other elements of the organizational balance model are not part of organizational cycling.

CHAPTER 2

Organizational Purpose

Where Strategy Comes From

The strategic management model that the average modern organization works to is not a new construct but instead finds its birthplace in the industrial revolution, which introduced the concept of man's endeavors being managed, measured, and mechanized and the workers being treated as if they were cogs in the machine of industry. This mechanistic foundation has impacted the development of organizations and management thinking, especially in the field of strategy. The suggested starting point for organization design is the setting of organization strategy. Strategic thinkers suggest many ways in which strategy may be formulated from a group of leaders sitting around designing where an organization is to go next, or, if you follow the learning school of strategy formation through a process of trial and error. Therefore, strategy can be created through planning, through an emergent process, or somewhere in between a planned or emerging process.

There is, however, a missing input in strategic management, or rather a failure to identify the true starting point of any organization. Strategic management speaks of where a strategy is formed but misses what it is formed from. What confounds good organizational design when beginning with strategy development is not who creates it or when is it created but rather where strategy creation begins. All industrial processes ultimately begin with natural resources; oil, water, minerals, and so on, and an idea of something that needs to be achieved. The puzzle, therefore, that the organization needs to solve is where strategy is created or rather where the idea of strategy appears, where, in all the managing, planning, or giving it a go of strategy that an organization must follow, do the ideas come from to decide what strategy an organization should be following. Perhaps, more importantly from a systems perspective, who decides what strategy is appropriate.

Purposeful Endeavor

The world has moved on from the industrial revolution concept of human endeavor. Human beings are not machines; if they are to perform in a sustainable way they cannot be standardized and put into boxes. If their potential is to be released, and an environment for sustainable performance is to be created, humans can't be treated as machines—they think, they feel, they are individual. Organizational Balance is achieved when the human elements within the organization are supported and encouraged to flourish with the organizational environment alongside the physical structures, processes, and systems.

In today's global context, the center of balance in an organization must start not with what must we do, but with why the organization exists. An organization must answer the question. "What is our purpose?" This is more than simply playing with semantics to choose the word purpose over strategy. There are so many terms used to describe the beginning of the strategic management process already and the words strategy, vision, mission, and purpose are often used interchangeably to mean the same thing. But the concept of purpose is extremely important in understanding the starting point of organization design from the perspective of the model of organizational balance. The *Oxford English Dictionary* defines purpose as "the reason for which something is done or created or for which something exists," whereas strategy is about a plan of action, vision is a plan for the future and a mission is an assignment. At an individual level, purpose is *being* rather than *doing*. When exploring the organization's purpose, the answer is not a profit number, or a growth percentage. Rather, purpose is at the very heart of reason why the organization exists, it is the beginning and the end "to make," "to deliver," "to achieve," "to create" or "to grow." Even then, the answer is not "to be number one" but rather to understand that if everything were to be stripped away and removed—structures, processes, products, and services—there would still be a reason for the organization to begin again. When all is said and done, it is what really *matters*.

Purpose is the oxygen of an organization's eco-system; without it, the organization will fail to create the center of organizational balance required for a sustainable environment in which it can perform at peak. Consider for a moment the physical performance required to climb a mountain where oxygen levels drop the higher up a mountaineer climbs. It is possible for the mountaineer to still keep going, but their ability to think and their physical performance levels will reduce the longer they are in an environment with low oxygen levels. It's not that an organization can't perform without clarity of purpose, but it will never achieve its full potential and performance will not be sustainable in the long term.

Finding Purpose

Finding purpose for an organization does not require a trip to a guru and months of chanting through the Chakras. The first thing that must be understood is that purpose is not created in the same way that strategy is created. Purpose is what it is. It is the answer to why the organization exists in the first place and it is the people in the organization who know better than anyone why an organization exists. Purpose isn't a top-down process. Finding purpose is inclusive, involving everyone from the cleaner through to the CEO who will all have something to contribute in regard to ideas about why the organization exists. To the cynical, this may sound fuzzy, gray, and wishy-washy. But if enough people are asked—whether a customer, a supplier, or an employee—what is this business about, the answers would be fairly consistent in regard to general direction. In my own experience, I once asked a manager at a well-known firm about their organization, and he stated quite confidently, "we're the tire people." The organization offered all kinds of services to a motorist but essentially the company existed because of tires. It may not have been a beautifully crafted statement of purpose, but the manager had captured the purpose of the organization in that one sentence.

Individuals who don't ask those very people who are part of the fabric of the organization what is the organizational purpose is missing the purpose of purpose. Purpose doesn't come from someone having an MBA or a hierarchical title because an organizational purpose isn't created. Rather, organizational purpose already exists in a temporal form and only need to be found or recognized.

Every organization will consist of employees who, if you were to cut them in half, would have the name of the organization written through them like Brighton Rock. The long-serving employees of the organization often have the life and the soul of the organization flowing through their veins and they are unashamed of their connection to what is the lifeblood of their place of work. Very often, these individuals are dismissed as being old school and not being able to keep up with the times. But like village elders they often have wisdom, which can be adapted and learned. It is this organization wisdom that preserves the heart of the organization, keeping it alive, even as how that heart is expressed changes. In many ways, it is the people who become the custodians of organizational purpose. This does not mean that individuals who have recently joined an organization can't understand its purpose. As with so many things in life, it is often the outsider who can see through the muck and bullets and give clarity when an organization has lost its way. An external perspective can be just as useful, and in seeking purpose, it is advisable that the organization listen to their external stakeholders and customers whose interaction with the organization in the marketplace is the outcome of its reason for existence.

Making the Unconscious Conscious

If for a moment we were to imagine that an organization were a person, which is made up of conflicting beliefs, thoughts, actions, and behaviors, it is possible to understand from where do challenges and opportunities arise and what shapes the thinking of the organization and why do organizations often become unbalanced. It is possible to bring the unconscious organization to the fore using various organizational diagnostic instruments and begin to understand why the organization operates in the way it does. This is no different from the premise that an individual will benefit from increasing their personal self-awareness, except that what is being raised is organizational awareness.

An individual can choose between being at the mercy of an event or being the cause, which is having a modicum of control over events. The same model can be applied to the organization as whole. By understanding why the organization exists in the first place and taking responsibility for being the cause of its actions, the organization will be able to take a modicum of control over the events which occur in the internal and external environment.

Benefits of Organizational Purpose

Research shows that employees feel they share the purpose of the organization if they believe that the organization wants them to contribute to shaping decisions. The shared experience an employee receives when understanding and relating to an organization's reason for existing produces a creative atmosphere of the possible. This is in contrast to the clunky organizational communication processes, which are more akin to selling the message than feeling part of what is happening.

Why Purpose Matters

Is it possible for an organization to be successful without having clarity around its purpose? Yes. Organizations have been and will continue to be successful without having a purpose. But the world is changing, and the pace of change is increasing. What used to define competitive advantage in regard to products, services, and capabilities has shifted from efficiency to effectiveness. Efficiency can be repeated, copied and adapted and is based on structures, processes, and hard systems. Effectiveness comes from utilizing knowledge, innovation, and creativity, which comes from people. People are unique and provide a critical element of competitive advantage for an organization.

Efficiency can be created without meaning being understood; it can be achieved by *doing* things better. But effectiveness requires people to have a sense of purpose in the activity they are pursuing, a reason for approaching a challenge differently, a reason for being the best they can be. For people to commit to the direction an organization is taking, they require an organization to have a meaningful purpose. Therefore, in the new global economy, the difference between an organization that can sustain performance and one that cannot will be the clarity of purpose which is shared among all employees.

This doesn't mean that organizations should throw out financial management, ignore the needs of the marketplace and get rid of key performance indicators. Organizations still need to do things better and to be doing the right things, but it is the purpose which aligns between these things and gives meaning to why doing things better and doing the right things is important to the organization and the individual employee.

Benefits of Organizational Purpose

In his book *The Purpose Driven Life*, Rick Warren (2002) sets out the benefits of having purpose. The benefits he outlines are as relevant to an organization as they are to an individual. The five benefits he identifies are as follows:

- *Purpose gives meaning to your life.* In the context of an organization, it gives meaning to what the organization sets out to achieve, giving what it does, even the occasional drabness of everyday working life significance and a hope for a better future. When difficulties come, as they often do, purpose will help overcome the challenges and succeed in taking advantage of opportunities. Purpose helps create the belief and drive that this organization *is* worth fighting for.
- *Purpose simplifies life.* Organizations are complex, and how often do we see leaders struggling to communicate a strategy, to get a message out there, understood and acted upon. "It defines what you do and what you don't do. Your purpose becomes the standard you use to evaluate which activities are essential and which aren't . . . Without a clear purpose you have no foundation on which you base decisions, allocate your time and use your resources" (Warren, 2002).
- *Purpose focuses your life.* If an organization is to create an environment for sustainable performance it needs to concentrate its energy and effort on what's important. Organizations very often go off at tangents and get distracted by issues or activities which are not relevant to its primary purpose. Focus will help prevent action which does not add value and wastes scarce resources.
- *Purpose motivates your life.* Where is an organization without passion for what it does? A clear purpose creates energy and sustains the passion that often wanes within an organization if people move on, or circumstances change. There are dozens of research studies which show the benefits of a motivated workforce in improving productivity and profitability.

- *Purpose prepares you for eternity.* Organizational life is often dictated by short-term issues and problems. Very few organizations survive in the long term as they go through difficult trading times: they are bought by competitors, are broken up, or they disappear. Having purpose leaves a legacy (Warren, 2002).

Purpose Improves Organizational Performance

Purpose is important because there is research evidence that purpose improves organizational performance. The Chartered Institute of Personnel and Development (CIPD) conducted a survey in December 2010 Shared Purpose; The Golden Thread, it showed that organizations which have purpose achieve better results in both financial measures such as profitability and people measures, including improved employee engagement and productivity.

Research studies conducted by Gallup have showed that engaged employees are 18 percent more productive, 12 percent more profitable and 60 percent less likely to leave the organization and take less time off sick (2.7 days per year versus 6.3 days for disengaged staff).

Going back to the eco-system analogy, if an organization fails to grow and change, adapting to the shifts in the environment in which it operates, it will die. But being able to change and adapt requires an organization to understand what it is in the first place, what its starting point is. Why an organization exists is the foundation stone upon which it can design structures and processes for its employees to build their capability to deliver organizational strategy. Purpose is the same as building with a solid, firm, and unshakable foundation, but without purpose an organization is unlikely to survive in the long term.

The result of a strong organizational purpose enables the workforce to focus on innovation, flexibility, and continuous improvement because they have a reason to pursue these things. This will give the organization competitive advantage over other businesses and the performance results will follow. Purposeful organizations enjoy sustainable growth and gain an enviable reputation with customers and suppliers. Although profits may be affected by the tough trading conditions and recession in the short term, purposeful endeavor ensures that the organization will continue to perform at a sustainable level and maintain competitive advantage regardless of market or industry conditions.

A Lesson from Marketing

A marketing professional has to, to a greater or lesser degree, grasp the concept of purpose when it comes to defining the products or services of the organizations they work for. Marketing describes not just the features and benefits of a product but also its purpose. It is a process that seeks to align the need for the business to make a profit through creating a relationship between the customer and the product or service on offer. If you consider some of the most memorable advertising, there is a connection to the purpose of the product or service that is being marketed which hooks us in as human beings, they define why what they are advertising matters, or should matter, to us—the consumer.

- It's the Real Thing—Coca Cola
- Be the First to Know—CNN
- The Best a Man Can Get—Gillette
- Because I'm Worth It—L'Oreal
- Just Do It—Nike
- The Future's Bright, The Future's Orange—Orange
- Reassuringly Expensive—Stella Artois

Good marketing relies on there being a purpose statement which forms the basis for all the marketing and customer communication activity; it is how the organization wishes to be perceived without all the creative marketing rhetoric. The purpose becomes the heart of the organization's product or service offering. A heartfelt purpose makes it much easier for the organization to create a marketing message that everyone will understand and connect with. If created and supported correctly, a marketing purpose statement will be a reflection of the overriding purpose of the organization as a whole.

Beware of Profit-Centered Purpose

Most executive teams, when questioned as to whether people are their number one priority in the business, will answer, of course yes. But on further questioning, they will eventually admit that actually people don't come first, profits do. It doesn't take much effort to research most organization's people practices to realize that this is the nature of most, though not all, organizations in operation today. Profit is king and their leaders pay lip service to people first. The problem with having profit as the core reason for an organization's existence is that the majority of employees in an organization don't care about a profit number. They may care when it comes to receiving their bonus if it is linked to the profit number. But hitting £80m profit or £1bn profit doesn't mean anything to the majority of the people who work for an organization. Individual employees in a firm cannot connect what they do on a day-to-day basis with a number; it has no meaning, no connection to their being.

For example, consider the last time you stayed in a hotel, can you remember your room number? Maybe, if you are reading this book in a hotel, you may know the number of the room you are staying in, or if it is a hotel room you stay in regularly or for long periods of time, then you might recall your hotel room number. But, for the majority of people, the number of the room and maybe even the hotel name probably escapes us.

Now think about the reason you last stayed at a hotel, the *purpose* of the hotel stay. It may have been for a conference, for a meeting, or a personal reason. When you think about the purpose of the stay, you can probably recall the room layout, the furniture, the bathroom decor, possibly even the food you ate. Human beings, even the most rational and logical of us, are better at focusing on something we can feel a connection to. For the vast majority of us we cannot feel a connection to a million or billion pound number, because we have no experience of what that means; it is meaningless.

In Shaping the Future research, the CIPD found that

> *Feelings towards profit-related purpose are generally negative, with employees saying it makes them feel de-motivated and less committed to their organization. Nonetheless, just under a third feels that*

*focusing on investors is the right thing to do in the long run. It seems
in order to produce a motivated and committed workforce, the main
purpose needs to have a social basis to it—profit does not seem to 'kick
start' the workforce (CIPD, 2010).*

Profit can also be confusing in a multinational organization. It may
have a specific growth ambition; for example, double the size of the business in 5 years. However, each division may have a growth ambition,
which is different from the organization as a whole. If each team has a different profit number, what, hope is there for the employees in the organization to have clarity on what the organization is trying to achieve. Speak
to any board of directors and they will discuss with you the difficulty they
have in communicating the strategy to the employees further down the
business, and how it gets diluted and lost in translation.

There is a story that I heard on the people development circuit about
a NASA employee who was sweeping the floor and was asked what his
job was, he answered it was to put a man on the moon; a purpose which
was articulated by John F. Kennedy in a statement in 1969. But even if
this story is nothing more than an urban myth, it illustrates the power
of purpose more than any other. The individual had purpose in what he
was doing, he wasn't doing some low-grade job, he was putting a man
on the moon. When I think about that story, I imagine the pride that
the employee must have put into his job, and how motivated he must
have felt when his alarm clock rang in the morning. Organizational purpose inspires purposefulness in employees and surely that is something all
organizations would want to aspire too?

This sense of purpose doesn't need expensive communication plans
or campaigns. It happens because individuals can connect to something
with meaning.

*Organizations can't impose a sense of shared purpose and manipu-
lated top-down selling of a common purpose creates cynicism and
resistance . . . By encouraging employees to find their own meaning at
work, they connect and create a true sense of what they are at work to
do, that's beyond profits or short-term efficiency measures and regardless of the sector they operate in (CIPD, 2011)*

There are many types of purpose that an organization can have rather than that of profit, but purpose broadly falls into two categories. The first is a societal purpose, which focuses on the contribution that the organization makes to society as a whole, such as being fair or acting with respect. The second category of purpose is one that defines human endeavor in terms of a business challenge such as quality or recognition as the best.

When a Purpose Becomes Invalid

The difference between an organization's purpose and strategy is that purpose will remain constant because it provides meaning throughout the years and to the multitudes of employees who pass through the organization's doors. An organization's strategy—the means by which an organization will work toward achieving its purpose—will change according to the current industry climate. However, sometimes an organization's *raison d'être* no longer fits with the external environment. This does not necessarily mean that an organization is on the endangered list and will eventually be extinct. Although an organization cannot evolve into something it is not, it does not mean that purpose is immovable, just that an organization can adapt their purpose overtime and with care.

Purpose may adjust over a period of time, and what an organization understands as its purpose will always be, but the articulation of its purpose will be clearer as organizational awareness and understanding grows. Events will also shape organizational purpose since events will impact the meaning of an organization's existence that had they not occurred, these events would have taken the organization on a different path.

Some events may be as a result of internal changes: innovations in product or service, changes in leadership or employees. Other events might be from the external environment. Without the introduction of the internet, organizations such as Amazon would not have a reason to exist, neither would the myriad of entrepreneurs and organizations that create web content. Other organizations may find purpose in tragedy or extraordinary opportunity. Events can and will create and shape purpose. Validity of existence can change and shift over the course of time. Purpose can change, but when it is does it will be felt within the employee population first. Again, the process of bringing the unconscious shift, which has taken place into a conscious articulation, is achieved through monitoring of where the organizational eco-system has changed.

The Role of Purpose and Organizational Balance

Like the human heart, organization's purpose is more than just the center of organization; it provides the lifeblood to the whole of the organizational system. It connects, refreshes, renews, and brings life to every single corner of the organization. If any part of the organization becomes disconnected from the purpose of the organization, it will wither and fail to function properly, like a limb cut from the body's blood supply. It is *impossible* to over-communicate with employees when sharing organizational purpose. For employees to own the organizational purpose they need to share the purpose, therefore creating mechanisms to explain how the organizational purpose relates to their day-to-day work is essential. Whether it is in meetings, one-to-ones, presentations, taglines on internal organizational literature, in employee briefings, newsletters, internal company magazines, social media, external press releases, posters, mouse mats, or even the screen saver on company computers; if it can be written, blogged, tweeted, spoken, mentioned, or referred to—do it.

Purpose and the Leader in Me

It is the leaders of the organization who will help create the clarity of organization purpose and provide the process by which organizational purpose is articulated, communicated, and role modeled. Without focused leadership, organizational purpose will get lost in the maelstrom of organizational activity, and strategic planning could take the organization away from its reason for existence. Leaders are the custodians of organizational purpose and responsible to ensure that the heart of the organization is maintained.

Purpose and the Talent Within

Organization's purpose connects the talent within the organization with the activities of the organization. Understanding the connection between the employees in an organization, the talent they possess and the talent required for the organizational purpose to be achieved creates the environment in which the individual employee's potential can be released. By creating an individual's job role around the talents they possess and aligning the talent to the needs of the organization, purpose provides the foundation for mapping the talent required while enabling the organization to support individuals in developing a self-awareness of how their talent can be used within the organizational setting and how they can develop their capability in line with organizational needs.

Purpose and Harmonious Communities

Purpose provides the glue by which individuals connect and group together. It provides the focus for relationship building and collaboration between individuals, teams, and functions collectively helping the organization pursue its purpose. Harmonious communities tap into the collective talent gathered from around the networked organization, making it is possible for the organization to expand from pockets of performance to an organization-wide sharing of expertise, knowledge, skill, and experience. Harmonious communities therefore enable organizational purpose to become meaningful, shared throughout the organization and translated into organizational activities.

Purpose and Organizational Habitat

The networked internal architecture is created to meet the change and challenge that internal and external influences will have on organizational activity in the pursuit of organizational purpose. At the same time it is the Organizational Habitat which provides a physical shape to the environment in which the organization's purpose is articulated. Organization Habitat can be compared with a person's home, which is both a reflection of and a springboard for their personality, achievements, hopes, and ambitions.

Purpose and Organizational Husbandry

Clarity of organizational purpose enables the organization to create the processes and practices and develop a methodology and methods of approaching the organizational resources sensitively. Through understanding why the organization exists, the organization can understand the consequences of its decisions and the impact those decisions will have on performance.

Organizational husbandry enables organizational purpose to fit within the internal organizational environment and find its place within the global economy, other corporations, and society as a whole.

Purpose and Creative Adaptation

Organizational purpose provides the focus and inspiration for creative thinking and innovation throughout organizational operations as the organizational leadership and individual employees pursue opportunities to succeed in achieving the purpose of the organization.

Creative adaptation feeds organizational purpose, enabling the reason for an organization to exist to adapt and adjust to the changes taking place in the external and internal environment.

Purpose and Energy Transformation

If organizational activity is going to add value to the organization, then organizational purpose provides the foundation for organizational activity to take place. Leaders and employees can ask themselves before taking action "does this help us achieve our purpose?" If it doesn't, then action can be suspended and time and resource (energy) is not wasted.

Out of the disorder of organizational activity, it is possible to create an understanding of the inputs and outputs of organizational activity and how internal and external environmental resources influence them. This understanding is part of the process of understanding organizational purpose and creating organizational strategy.

Summary

- The center of balance in an organization must start not with what must we do, but with why the organization exists.
- You do not *create* purpose in the same way that you create strategy. Purpose is what it is. It is the answer to why the organization exists in the first place.

- Research shows that employees feel that they share the purpose of the organization if they believe that the organization wants them to contribute to shaping decisions.
- For people to commit to the direction an organization is taking, they require an organization to have a meaningful purpose.
- Organizational purpose provides five benefits:
  - Purpose gives meaning to your life
  - Purpose simplifies life
  - Purpose focuses your life
  - Purpose motivates your life
  - Purpose prepares you for eternity
- Organizations that have purpose achieve better results in both financial measures such as profitability and people measures including improved employee engagement and productivity.
- Purpose broadly falls into two categories. Societal purpose and one that defines human endeavor in terms of a business challenge.
- Purpose will remain constant because it provides meaning, but events can and will create and shape purpose.

Organizational purpose provides the lifeblood to the whole of the organizational system.

CHAPTER 3

The Leader in Me

People can provide a competitive advantage only if they are both well led and well managed.

—Edward Lawler III

On Leadership

Fifty years ago, managers were put in the position to manage the employees of the organization because of what or who they knew; their social status or technical ability was a precursor to achieving promotion to a managerial position. Everyone who entered an organization knew that if they worked hard enough, got on with the right people, and stuck around long enough, eventually they too would be promoted and would achieve the title of manager. The world has moved on, but it would seem that the expectation that at some point everyone is able to get promoted to be in "the management" hasn't. The difference is that it is no longer decades that individuals are willing to wait; 2 years' service and ambitious individuals will begin questioning why they have not taken a step up the next rung of the career ladder.

More often than not, organizations will promote an individual because of their accomplishments in their current role, for example, in the sales arena, a sales representative who brings in a lot of revenue will be given the role of sales manager because the individual wants to be recognized for the contribution they are making and the organization wants to reward the individual with a bigger role within the organization. The problem is that without understanding the capability of the individual to lead people, this process often does not work. The organization rarely has the procedures in place to assess whether the individual has the necessary disposition to lead a group of people effectively, and there are few organizations that offer career paths available to manage the careers of talent based on experience or expert knowledge without line management responsibility within the organization setting.

In the modern organization, what defines a good manager or leader is no longer connected to what technical knowledge you have, because there is too much information, knowledge, and data for a manager of a department to know it all. Over the past 50 years, the management paradigm has shifted to that of coaching, support, and empowerment, resulting in a two-way leader–follower process. Today, organizations require flexibility and fluidity not just in how leadership is viewed and practiced in the organizational setting, but also in the possible leadership career paths available if it is to positively influence individual and organization performance.

Why Effective Leadership Is Important

Whatever the organization, regardless of its culture, it is through the leadership process that the efforts of employees are coordinated, given direction, and moved toward the achievement of the organization's purpose. It is the leadership in the organization that will integrate the activity of the employees and provide a linchpin for creating the environment for sustainable performance.

Leadership of an organization's workforce is effective in a wider context of the global economy which includes shifting attitudes toward work and changes in the way organizations interact with their customers, suppliers, shareholders, and competitors. As we move forward, change is a constant, being driven by a more aggressive competitive setting, a more demanding customer base, scientific, engineering, and technological advances and the requirement for greater adaptability and flexibility.

Leader or Manager

There is a lot of literature and research focused on the difference between a leader and a manager with the definitions giving varying descriptions based on the theme that leaders provide a vision and direction and managers are involved in the planning, implementation, and allocation of resources.

The issue with this formal separation is identifying the leader and the manager in a modern organization. The situation in most organizations is that there are managers who lead and leaders who also manage.

Fortunately, nothing about being a good manager prevents somebody from being a good leader, and nothing about being a good leader prevents somebody from being a good manager. Indeed, the behaviours that go along with being a good manager and being a good leader are typically quite complementary (Lawler III, 2008).

The difference between those defined as leaders or managers is not so much in what the individual concerned does—planning or directing—but rather who the individual *is*.

For the purposes of this book, the term leader will be used, but this can also be read as Manager. The concern is not what someone does in the organization or what their job title is but rather who that person is, hence the title of this section—The Leader in Me.

Spotting a Leader

Not everyone can be a leader and leaders are neither born nor made. They are both born *and* made. There are two distinct types of leaders: leaders of people and leaders of expertise. There may be some individuals who are blessed with being both a leader of people and a leader of expertise, but these are rare.

This distinction is important in creating an environment for performance, getting leadership wrong can cause serious damage to the organization and the consequences of poor leadership can be fatal to the performance of individuals under a leader's remit and to the leaders' own performance. It can destroy people and environments. A misplaced leader can have a similar effect as introducing a nonnative species to an environment. It has unintended and sometimes devastating consequences.

The challenge for organizations and for leaders in an organization is in developing a self-awareness of the leadership type of an individual or whether they are cut out to be a leader at all. Too often individuals are promoted because they are too good to lose, or because they feel they have to show a willingness to progress in order to get the recognition or the pay rise they crave. The proposal is that organizations begin to recognize leaders of expertise, promoting them commensurate with the responsibilities they hold in their area of expertise, rather than forcing talented individuals to manage people. Rewarding leaders for continuing to develop their expertise would mean that businesses would not have to worry about losing their best minds, knowledgeable and experienced individuals. Having a route of promotion based on expertise would enable individuals to achieve the recognition and career development they desire without doing something that is not within their talent capability.

It is worth noting that leadership teams are normally made up of people in leadership roles. This has an incredibly limiting impact on the successful environment of a business; it means possible leadership success to those with a specific skills set and talent. In the context of an organization, the leadership hierarchy consists of leading teams of people. Quite often, individuals are trained in several areas to learn people skills, which lead to two things: either they sink because their people skills are so poor that the individual implodes or does their team or they have enough people skills to do an adequate job, but their leadership in their area of expertise is too important for the organization to lose so the organization tolerates poor people management.

The unintended consequence is that the leader is unable to perform effectively. People management takes up too much of their time so they have less time to focus on their field of expertise and at the same time, the people they lead are unable to perform effectively because of how they are being led.

Case Study—Santander

Santander is operating in a rapidly changing environment and has ambitious growth and performance plans geared to becoming a full-service commercial bank and the best bank in the UK. With these priorities, it is essential that they can ensure the depth and continuity of corporate leadership talent in all its forms. As a retail bank, Santander works with a highly regulated environment that requires a wide range of specialist "back office" expertise, such as finance, risk, compliance, and legal. However, at heart, Santander remains a people business, servicing over 25 million customers, running over 1,300 branches, and optimizing the abilities and aspirations of over 27,000 employees. Within this context, Santander have become well versed in the need to recognize, develop, and optimize both "experts" and "people leaders". However, despite these being two distinct career routes (or preferences), Santander uses a common approach and strategy right from job evaluation through to reward.

The initial starting point is around job and organizational design. Santander uses a common role profile format that clearly lays out the accountabilities of the role, the competencies required, and the necessary qualifications, experience, or training to be successful in the role. At this early stage, Santander is able to identify which of these roles require specialist expertise or where the role is primarily around people management. As a generalization, the front office functions in Santander are heavily reliant on strong people skills, for example, branch managers while the back office functions require more specialist expertise such as marketing, risk, and compliance. All the job roles in Santander are formally evaluated and sized and it is at this point that Santander considers different elements of a role, such as the complexity of any team management, the impact on business results, and the complexity of the market.

The organizational structure is flexible enough to take into account where individual strengths lie. Historically, it has not been unusual to see very expert areas having a chief operating officer role that would take on more of the leadership and people management duties in order to leave specialists to focus on their particular areas. However, all senior managers are expected to be leaders—regardless of whether they manage people. All leaders are expected to be competent and self-improving, even if their preference is to focus solely on their specialist area. The ability to build relationships, to motivate and inspire others, and to drive strong performance is something that Santander demands in all their managers. Once in a role, Santander offers a strong talent and development management process that enables the organization to look at a role and an individual and to plan the necessary development. There is an increased move to building career paths for junior colleagues so that they can easily access materials and support that will enable them to develop in the way that best meets their abilities and aspirations. So even as an early stage in their career, Santander provides progression routes into management or alternative routes into a more technical or expert stream.

At more senior levels, Santander invests heavily in building talent identification and management processes. They have committees in place that review each of the senior managers in terms of their background, track record, strengths and development areas, potential and aspirations to ensure that individuals develop and progress in ways and into roles that meet their aspirations and the demands of the business. The same process is used whether an individual wishes to follow a generalist, specialist, or management career route. Santander understands that when they understand the needs of the business and the impact that has on their leadership needs, which will be for a mixture of people managers, generalists, and expert specialists, they can use their talent processes to ensure that the appropriate skills are in place and rewarded and supported in a way that drives high performance (Curtis, 2011).

Leaders of People

Whether it is in coaching for performance, giving and receiving feedback, managing remote teams, or performance management, the list of skills and behaviors that businesses want their leaders to master is endless and growing. One thing is clear; there is an established recognition in organizations that being a good leader of people requires people with *soft* skills and different behaviors to enable employee engagement, motivation, and performance. But no matter how many workshops and away days some individuals attend, they still seem to pull up short when it comes to achieving the team performance they want to create.

Employees cannot be owned by the organization in the same way that its capital resources can be. Individuals bring with them their own worldviews, attitudes, and behavior that interact with the organization in a unique and individual way. Being able to lead people requires an ability to think in terms of the collective and demonstrate an ability to balance the needs of the individual with those of the organization.

The reason for the distinction between a leader of people and a leader of expertise is because fundamentally it is a mistake to think that just because you can be taught *people* skills you can lead people, just like it is a mistake to believe that just because you can be taught engineering skills you can become an engineer or be taught the skills of playing tennis you can become a tennis player.

This doesn't mean that organizations should cancel all future people skills workshops and development away days. Quite the opposite, because those who *are* leaders of people must learn how to hone their natural talent for leading people and improve their people skills to become the best leader of people they can be at releasing the people capability and drive collaboration in team of people to perform. This is no different from an organization investing in training their IT teams in IT skills, and customer service teams in customer service. The step change organizations need to make is that people skills learning interventions will be targeted at those people who have the talent to lead people in the first place.

Identifying a Leader of People

Leaders of people may also be individuals who have expertise in some areas, but more often than not they can work in several areas of expertise but are not necessarily *Expert* experts. A leader of people has within them an authority and gravitas that comes from inside. It can't be learned, or faked. They are the people who when they speak, people listen to, not because what they say is any better or worse than the next person but because of the way they hold themselves, the way they engage with people they are talking to and the tone, inflection, and timbre of their voice. They engage on a personal level and they make the people they are leading feel like they are important.

Leaders of people may sometimes feel they have a conflicting appointment, between the competing needs of different stakeholders: their employees, the organization, the customers, the suppliers, regulators, and so on. But it is the talent of managing these conflicts in a way that aligns their employee's purpose and talent with the needs of the organization and the organization's stakeholders that makes an individual a leader of people. The leader of people is the bridge between the organization and the individual employees. They must skillfully manage the differing interests and goals of the different individuals and groups within the organizational setting and manage any conflict in a proactive and positive way.

A leader of people also finds a fulfillment of their own purpose in understanding and motivating other people, developing a network, building relationships, and making a difference in other people's lives. Their passion for helping release people to be the best they can be is an expression of their personal purpose. It doesn't mean that a leader of people does not want to achieve personal goals or targets, but it is gaining that achievement through other people that they find most satisfying. Good leaders of people can identify how to marry the individual desires and goals of their employees with the requirements of the organization in achieving its purpose and strategy. By connecting on a personal level with their employees, the leader of people is able to spot potential for creative use of skills, experience, behaviors, and talent that enables the individual to spend most of their time working in areas in which they can be their best and release their talent potential. In doing so, the leader of people tunes the employee to the right activities in the organization like tuning a radio to the right frequency. Leaders of people also have the ability to engender confidence and loyalty because they show genuine concern for the people that they lead. They continually demonstrate a willingness to listen to the ideas and input of those around them. They have the ability to make others feel their contribution is valued and are secure enough in their own abilities to proactively develop those around them.

Leaders of people have a clear set of personal principles such as integrity, honesty, treating others with respect, and loyalty, which they demonstrate in their daily activity and articulate purposefully. In addition to acting in line with their own principles, they also create an environment where those around them have the freedom to express themselves. The leader of people is able to listen to an individual and gain understanding of what is important to that individual. In understanding what drives the individuals under their leadership remit, the leader then creates the opportunity for that individual to express themselves and their principles when tackling the work tasks they have been allocated.

Leaders of Expertise

Although most operational leaders will be required to have strategic and people skills in other areas, it will be necessary for organizations to find individuals who have the ability to convert the knowledge that is in the business, giving it a fresh perspective and injecting fresh thinking. The increasing importance of the knowledge worker in the organizational environment has created a greater awareness of the importance of the knowledge, expertise, and innovative thinking as a source of competitive advantage.

In the same way as it is important to be a leader of people in order to deliver performance through people, it is a mistake to think that just because you are able to lead people you can lead an area of expertise. You might be able to inspire individuals and bring teams together, but that does not mean you are able to understand critical areas of knowledge, development, or thinking. This distinction is usually more obvious, or rather clichéd, in technical fields such as science, technology, engineering, and math. Very often it is individuals who lack, often painfully, people skills, whose expertise and leadership in their field has not only helped organizations have the edge over competitors but have enabled humankind to be all it is in today's modern world—for good and bad.

In the knowledge economy, organizations must recognize that leadership talent comes in a number of forms that cannot be constrained by a single model of leadership, but require recognition of those individuals who have the expertise to be promoted into specialist leaders of expertise roles. For a leader of expertise to develop in their area of expertise, they must network with other experts in their field. Networking within the organizational setting is only part of the puzzle. To ensure their expertise remains current and is in line with best practice, not just in their industry but also in the global context, they must learn to connect and network effectively with other experts outside their organization.

Identifying Leaders of Expertise

In most organizations, leaders of expertise can be hidden from view. They are individuals who sometimes have difficulty remaining visible and establishing the right profile to be perceived as a future leader. In the organizations where they are spotted and their contribution valued by the organization, they are promoted out of jobs that they enjoy and excel and into roles that they don't have the skills for.

Very often they become the go-to person for individuals within the organization on specific topics of expertise and knowledge. They may or may not be great with people, but their keen interest in their area of expertise can be likened more to that of a hobby than a job. Their ability to understand new information in the context of their area of expertise, make connections between information, and apply their knowledge and understanding to task at hand can be relied upon regardless of who they are working with or what task they are being required to complete. Being able to translate their expertise into the day-to-day requirements of organizational tasks and goals is important if a leader of expertise is going to be able to apply what they know in the organizational context. Mentoring is a key skill that can add real value by giving access to expertise through answering questions and giving advice.

It is no use the leader of expertise being an expert if that expertise cannot be applied to the achievement of the organizational purpose. Although the leader of expertise does not need the same communication skills that a leader of people requires, they do need to be able to translate their expertise in a way that can be understood by those with whom they work. Translating what they know and understand into something that other people can use is an essential skill if the leader of expertise is to use their knowledge in the organizational setting.

The leadership team should be made up of both leaders of people and leaders of expertise. If the CEO is a leader of people, they will benefit from including a leader of expertise in their direct team. Likewise, if the CEO is a leader of expertise, ensuring that a leader of people is a right-hand man/woman will enable them to lead the organization effectively. Without both types of leader in the leadership team, organizational balance will not be possible. Too much emphasis on people will mean that competitive advantage from expert knowledge will remain unharnessed; too much emphasis on expertise and the engagement of the workforce will suffer. Either scenario is equally catastrophic for the creation of sustainable performance.

Case Study—Barclay Meade

Barclay Meade is one of the UK's leading professional staffing recruitment agencies dealing with permanent and temporary recruitment solutions in accountancy, financial services, human resources, procurement, supply chain and logistics, sales, marketing and communications, and executive search.

A couple of years ago, Barclay Meade changed the career management structure for leaders to include both a management route and a lead consultant route. Each route offered the same benefit package, but only the management route required direct people management. Those who followed the lead consultant route became Best Practice champions on topics relevant to the business. They have the expertise and become the go-to person in the business for critical areas of expertise. For example, CRB checks for immigration point scoring.

The reason for the change was prompted by the performance management system. When having open and honest conversations with people about why they worked at Barclay Meade and what their goals were, many people talked about the fact that they liked the business, industry, direction, and so on, and that was more important to them than becoming the next chief executive. The result was the Barclay Meade began to map out a personal development and career plan for each individual centered around their goals, which placed an emphasis on experience and acquiring an in-depth expertise area, based upon what enthused or interested the individual.

Everyone likes hugely knowledgeable and expert people in their teams, especially new line managers. The experts have become the new line managers back up in getting things done. The expert is required to promote competence as a team player and support and mentor junior managers.

The result is leaders of expertise who feel valued and recognized, celebrated, and rewarded drawing out those who are suited to a supervisory or a nonsupervisory role. The transparent career and visible promotional paths have enabled Barclay Meade to retain good people, which they may otherwise have lost to other organizations, improved knowledge retention and sharing around the group through the creation of expert experts and has had a positive contribution to the business (Roe, 2011).

The Importance of Purposeful Leadership

All leaders should believe that what they do has meaning. All leaders should have purpose. The purpose that a leader has will not necessarily be the same as organizational purpose; in fact, it is highly unlikely that their personal purpose is exactly the same as that of the organizational purpose since the reasons why an organization exists will be different from the reason why an individual believes they have been put on this planet.

> *While the research identifies the importance of communications and leadership in developing a sense of shared purpose, what emerges is that employees surveyed particularly believe that senior leaders, board members and trustees must clearly demonstrate that they too live the values. This 'on board' attitude from senior management also has the ability to improve job satisfaction—respondents who feel senior management keep the organization purpose at the heart of their visions and strategies are more likely to be satisfied with their job than those who do not (CIPD, 2010).*

It may be that they believe that they are able to galvanize and lead a team to achieve organizational purpose. Or like myself as a development professional, I believe that I can help an organization achieve its purpose through my area of expertise. Or it may be for entirely different reasons. But if a leader is not able to express their personal purpose in the organizational setting, they will be unable to perform effectively over a period of time and if their personal purpose does not in some way align with that of the organization you may find that the leader begins to pull in a direction that is different from the requirements of the organization.

As part of the selection process, it is important that organizations have frank conversation with individuals about what they wish to achieve and what their purpose is, first, to understand how the organization can help the leader be purposeful in their day-to-day activities but, second, to ensure that the alignment between the organization and the individual purpose is meaningful.

The Role of Leadership in Organizational Balance

Organizations love processes. It makes things easy to replicate, it means that mass production and forecasting are possible. The problem is processes can't be built around individuals, because no two people are the same, the way they respond to world around them, to the stimuli in their immediate environment will be different from someone else and the consequences of their response will not always fit into a tidy framework.

In individualistic approach, not only are the individual's talents and needs considered but also the situational aspects of the leadership role that the individual is being considered for. For example, Winston Churchill is probably considered one of the most successful prime ministers in UK history, but his leadership talent was linked to the wartime situation the country was facing at the time. By the time peace came, Churchill's leadership talent no longer suited the situation in which he was trying to lead. Therefore, from an organization design perspective, a better approach would be to concentrate on the leader the individual is and how that fits into the leadership capability required by the organization. Job descriptions and competencies concentrate on performance reviews on the negative framing of what someone is not doing or what someone doesn't have. Development plans improve areas of weakness, not areas of strength.

> *Great managers would offer you this advice: Focus on each person's strengths and manage around his weaknesses. Don't try to fix weaknesses. Don't try to perfect each person. Instead do everything you can to help each person cultivate his talents. Help each person become more of who he already is (Buckingham, 1999).*

Connecting leaders with their personal passions, values, and purpose means that sustainable leadership performance can be achieved. A leader must develop processes to recognize, understand, and self-assess their talent, potential, and abilities and the internal resources and limits that they can pull on in any work situation.

This idiographic approach offers a holistic approach to discover the leader in a person. It requires leaders to take an account of their whole self when examining their motivations, career ambitions, and the way they relate, not just to the team they lead, but also to their own peers and superiors. This process is continuous, since an individual is not static and develops and changes as their life journey shapes them.

The Leader in Me and Purpose

Clarity of organizational purpose will establish the leadership capability that the organization requires to achieve its current plans and its future plans and strategy. The purpose will enable the leaders of people to understand the direction in which the organization is heading, and therefore the direction in which they need to lead their followers. In regard to the leaders of expertise, the organizational purpose will give clarity and provide direction in regard to the areas of expertise that they must develop and the internal and external networks, which will be essential in helping the organization, be successful. Purpose creates the areas in which leaders will be responsible, in order to achieve their own tasks and their contribution to the creation of an environment of sustainable performance. Organizational purpose provides the relay through which the leadership process will flow to ensure that the efforts of employees are coordinated, given direction, and their activity integrated, providing a linchpin for creating the environment for sustainable performance.

The Leader in Me and the Talent Within

The influence on sustainable performance between Leaders and the Talent Within is twofold. First, in regard to the talent that the individual leader has and how their talent is used by the organization to add value, and second, in respect to how leaders enable the Talent Within the organization to flourish. Leaders of people are the custodians of Talent Within the organization, in the sense that the way in which they lead those reporting to them will impact an individual employees' ability to perform and be the best that they can be. Leaders of Expertise contribute to the release of individual potential, including that of their leadership colleagues, by being the custodians of knowledge and expertise in the organization, which can be used by individuals to perform at their best. Even though leaders of expertise may not have direct people management responsibility, their role in mentoring and supporting individuals in the business is crucial if the Talent Within is to be released.

The Leader in Me and Harmonious Communities

Leaders and employees need to work together to create the environment that encourages and facilitates individuals and teams and functions to build relationships and collaborate in order to collectively help the organization pursue its purpose. The leaders enable information, knowledge, communication, and relationship to flow through the organization. Disruption to this flow can occur if there are weak points in the leadership network. The informal groups and communities that form within the organization influence the leadership of the organization due to the development of their own leadership and hierarchy. Recognizing these informal groups will influence and contribute to the leadership pipeline within the organization.

The Leader in Me and Organizational Habitat

The foundation of traditional leadership power based on organizational hierarchy does not facilitate the development of leadership talent based on either people skills or expertise, which delivers competitive advantage for the organization. The design of the organizational structure is required to be more flexible to allow for individual leadership talent and collaboration and relationships among teams to flourish. Traditional hierarchical structures would inhibit the development of career paths for leaders of expertise to be recognized and promoted based on the contribution that they bring to the organization. The networked organization will remove the barriers that would normally prevent contribution and added value from being recognized as leadership talent.

The leadership has a significant contribution to make in regard to the establishment of an open environment in which individuals are empowered to collaborate and build relationships across the networked organization. The development of transitory project groups and support cross functionally will only occur if the leadership teams allow them to happen.

Role modeling of collaborative behaviors in the workplace and developing networking skills will have a considerable impact on the effectiveness of leadership within the organization.

The Leader in Me and Organizational Husbandry

Organizational processes and practices, such as those for performance management, reward and recognition, career management and succession planning and personal development opportunities, directly impact the effectiveness of the contribution that leadership can make to the creation of an environment for sustainable performance. Should these practices be based on a flawed methodology, the leader will be restricted in releasing their full potential. In the same way, the leadership team is ultimately responsible for how organizational resources are coordinated and used within the organizational setting. The way in which they manage and provide direction based on the changes both internally and externally to the organization will affect the performance environment. Leaders who do not understand the consequences of their decisions could be devastating to the organization and individual employees.

The Leader in Me and Creative Adaptation

The leadership team is critical in establishing a culture of creativity within the organizational setting. By proactively pursuing the use of creativity, innovation, and critical thinking in solving challenges and identifying opportunities as part of day-to-day organizational activity, leaders create the environment where creativity and innovation are considered the norm.

The culture of the organization will impact the behaviors and expectations of the leadership team and employees within the organization. An organizational environment, which promotes creative adaptation, will demand a leadership team that empowers individuals to make decisions and encourages out-of-the-box thinking. This too will affect the leadership team themselves, who also need to think differently about the changes that the organization faces. Strategic management and tactical planning must give room for adaptation and flexibility, and this requires leaders to lead the organization proactively.

The Leader in Me and Energy Transformation

Leaders are at the forefront of evaluating how the inputs and outputs of organizational activity are contributing to overall organizational performance. The strategy and plans that the leaders enact should be aligned to the organizational purpose. When planning organizational activity, the leadership team should establish criteria for measuring success. Leaders should consider what measures can be used to demonstrate the value added from the time and resource committed and what success would look like from the activities planned.

Through the evaluation of the energy transformation, the effectiveness of the leadership team in directing the activities of the organization and creating an environment for sustainable performance will be revealed. The results of the evaluation of energy transformation should highlight areas where the leadership needs to change direction or improve focus on an area of resource allocation to improve the impact that activities have on the achievement of organizational purpose.

Summary

- It is through the leadership process that the efforts of employees are coordinated, given direction and moved toward the achievement of the organization's purpose.
- The difference between those defined as leaders or managers is not so much in what the individual concerned does—planning or directing—but rather in who the individual *is*.
- There are two distinct types of leadership: leaders of people and leaders of expertise.
- Leaders of people can identify how to marry the individual desires and goals of their employees with the requirements of the organization in achieving its purpose and strategy.
- In the knowledge economy, organizations must recognize that leadership talent comes in a number of forms and requires recognition of those individuals who have the expertise to be promoted into specialist leadership roles.

CHAPTER 4

The Talent Within

While experience, brainpower, and willpower all affect performance significantly, only the presence of the right talents—recurring patterns of behaviour that fit the role—can account for this range of performance. Only the presence of talents can explain why, all other factors being equal, some people excel in the role and some struggle.

—Marcus Buckingham

The Talent Within

The War on Talent and the rise of Talent Management processes within organizations speaks of a world where the talent resource held by people within the workplace is being recognized as a key competitive advantage. But too often senior leaders declare that, yes, people are important or employees must come first and yet, sadly, too often the way that an organization treats and manages it's "most important asset" is in stark contrast to the declarations of importance.

It could be argued that leaders are lying about their intent when it comes to people. So often they pour over profit and loss statements and balance sheets looking at how to get a better return on investment and yet their people practices are never examined in the same detail to ensure that their people assets are performing to their full potential. Consider, for example, talent management practices that focus on the top 10 percent of identified employee talent, shareholders would be calling leaders to account in the AGM if their business practices only sought to develop and improve 10 percent of their capital assets.

Developing people and discovering and releasing the talent within does not have to be expensive, but it does need attention. Senior leadership teams spend a significant percentage of their time examining, planning, and strategizing over the assets of the business, but there are few action plans, meetings, telephone calls, and emails purely examining the people and talent asset in a business. Few senior leaders would have a deep knowledge of the talent within the organization compared to how well they know the return on capital employed or the percentage return on asset; they know the balance sheet better than they know the people who work in the organization. Despite the number of books, papers, and studies completed on workplace psychology and human resource management the full potential of capital investment fails, or at least fails to be as successful as it could be. Building awareness of talent potential and developing plans in the business to release the talent within need to extend beyond the immediate top team and leadership succession plans.

Spending millions on business processes, or information systems and completely failing to invest in ensuring that they are aligned to people processes or ensure that work is completed so that the people who use the processes or systems have the capability to respond positively to the change taking place must be part of the organization design process. The importance of talent within the organization's design cannot be underestimated.

Why Is Engaging the Talent Within so Important?

People are what make an organization. A bad process and even a poor product can still be overcome with the right people. But the right people need to have the right capability for the organization they work for. Too often, highly talented individuals are unsuccessful because they are either in the wrong job role or in the wrong organization. We all know for ourselves that we are most successful when we are given the space and the opportunity to do what we are good at. And when that opportunity is given, we give more of ourselves because we feel fulfilled in doing so; these things must not and cannot be underestimated. Employee engagement and talent management may seem like yet more HR jargon, the latest buzzwords. However, the reason for the noise surrounding employee engagement is because that it allows significant competitive advantage: "Research carried out by the Hackett Group in 2007 shows that companies that have effective talent management systems, as opposed to those that don't, have earnings that are 15 percent higher, net profit margins that are 22 percent higher, ROA is 49 percent higher, and ROE that is 27 percent higher" (Stuart-Kotze, 2008).

Engaging the talent of only a small percentage of people in an organization or focusing on a high potential or future leaders program is inadequate. Every single individual within the organization has talent, and organizations must know how to discover and release the talent within the organization; individuals must understand and be able to utilize the talent within themselves if sustainable performance is to be achieved.

Defining Talent

Too often talent can be confused with genius or what society has deemed to be extraordinary ability or skill in an area of publicly recognized pursuit, such as sport or music. But talent is so much more complex and yet ordinary than pure ability. Too often talent is described as a gift, as if only certain people have the capacity to be talented. But that is not true. Everyone single individual is extraordinarily unique and, as such, each person has an extraordinary talent. However, most individuals wouldn't know what their talent was if it came and hit them over the head. The reason is that an individual's talent ultimately makes them *talented* at something; which means we probably don't notice that what we do is amazing, because it is just something we are able to do; and the stuff that comes easy to us doesn't seem that extraordinary. Foster, Moore, and Stokes (2014) defined talent "as knowledge, skills or ability that an individual or organization perceives as recognizable capability that has intrinsic value" and identified determinants of talent: perception and context.

Your Talent

Consider for yourself what it is that you are able to do without much effort. Your talent within is that ability you have (mental, physical, social) which you can just do, when if asked how you do it, you can't actually break down into steps because you just do it. Take David Beckham. He had the same coaching and training as many top footballers, but it is his ability to place a ball anywhere he likes on a football field that stands him apart from his contemporaries. That "talent" can't be taught as a skill, it can't be practiced as experience and it has nothing to do with the way in which David Beckham behaves. The skills, experience, and behaviors enhance his talent and help release its potential, but his talent—that was there from the day he was born. Now think about the people in your organization. Maybe there is an administrator who can be relied on to keep things organized; the salesperson who consistently delivers on target, although they may never have been salesperson of the year; the customer services representative who has never had a customer complaint; the engineer whose services never fail. These people might not be extraordinary in terms of genius talent, but they deliver consist performance and they demonstrate talent day in day out because of the ease with which they do their job role.

Consider then those who are underperforming, the people who may be are not suited in the role they perform. It isn't that they lack talent, it is that in their present role their talent isn't being used.

In the book *Who Are Your Best People* it defines talent as "the ability and capability to do something well." It goes on to say that "Talent has two components: ability (current performance) and capability (potential performance). Ability is about the now; capability is about the future. Both can be observed, tested and measured" (Stuart-Kotze, 2008). This perhaps highlights the difference between performance and talent because everyone has the capacity to do something well, it just may not yet be discovered.

Therefore, in order for organizational balance to be achieved, it is important that time is spent on clarifying the talent (ability and capability) the organization requires now and in the future to achieve its purpose; that processes are in place to identify the talent within the organization; that employees understand the talent within themselves; that structures and processes are in place to enable people to release and develop their potential, and that the recruitment and selection process is focused on attracting and identifying talent which the organization needs when it needs it.

The Talent Required Within

Understanding the talent required is essential for organizational balance to be achieved. Focusing on developing purposeful and effective talent management, leadership teams must understand critical talent ability and capability required to achieve organizational purpose and design and develop strategies to ensure the organization can recruit, retain, and develop the talent it needs today to deliver performance now and in the future. "Finding, acquiring, and retaining the right talent is a necessary, but not a sufficient, step in creating an organization with a sustainable competitive advantage. To do this, an organization also has to have the right structures, systems, processes, and practices in place. All too often, organizations have great people but do not manage or support them correctly. People are stifled by systems and processes that restrict experimentation, limit learning, hinder the transfer of knowledge, fail to motivate, and suppress innovation. As a result, organizations fail to capitalize on the talent they have and in the long run perform poorly" (Lawler III, 2008).

It is not enough for leaders to develop a resource plan, which sets down job tasks that need to be completed and outlines the skills that individuals need to be able to do. Organizational design requires a talent process that matches the talent requirements to strategic plans. The strategy requires more than a list of skills, experience, or behavioral competencies, but an identification of the types of talent that will provide the organization with the ability and capability to achieve its purpose. Identification of talent is as important as any other investment decision that an organization will make. Understanding exactly what type of talent the organization has and what talent it needs to invest in is as important, if not more so as making investment decisions in other capital projects.

At the heart of this process is the organization's purpose. Developing a talent identification system, which outlines a clear set of criteria against which talent performance can be measured and which is clear and objective, is the foundation stone upon which the talent management process within the organization sits.

The Expanded Boundaryless Talent Model

In Foster (2017b) describes the Expanded Boundaryless Talent Model (Figure 4.1) as follows:

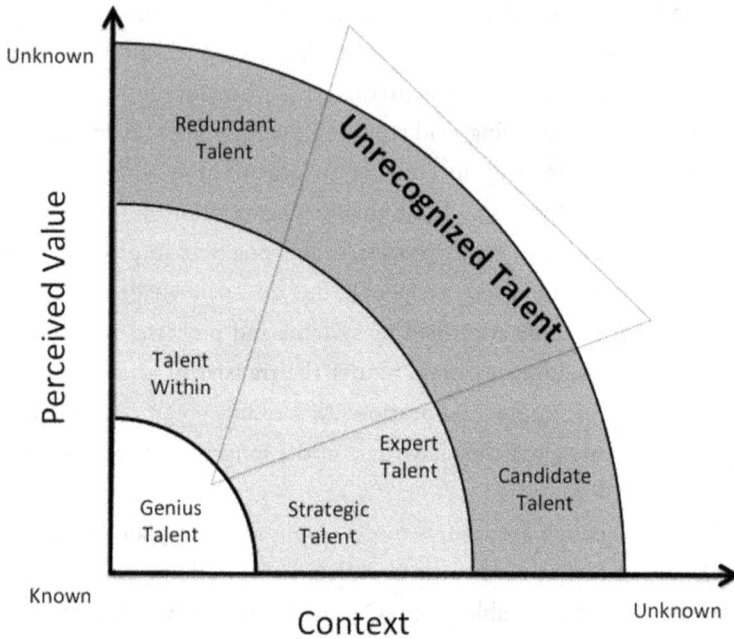

**Figure 4.1 The boundaryless talent management model
(Foster, 2017b)**

Perceived Value—Expanded BTM

The perceived value of talent may be unknown in regard to what talent is required in the future either due to changes in organizational strategy or in response to disruptive changes in the external environment such as new technology, products, services, markets, processes, and so on. Since organizational leaders do not know with certainty what is needed, they may discard talent today that may at a later date develop a perceived value.

It could be argued that talent is subject to fashion and fad, as much as any other human endeavor. Furthermore, talent can reduce in perceived value if enough people acquire a skill, knowledge, or ability for it no longer to be extraordinary. For example, before the printing press, and universal education, being able to read and write was highly valued, whereas in today's world, lacking literacy skills results in a perception of inferiority. In the 1960s, computer programming and software development were on par with secretarial work and relegated to a woman's work—a far cry from the male-dominated professional programmers of today (Eveleth, 2013).

Talent Context—Expanded BTM

The context axis of the Expanded BTM refers to the known or unknown context in which talent resides. From an organizational leader's perspective, the more they know about the context, the more certain they will be as to whether the talent is needed or not within the organization. Talent that exists outside the organization is an unknown quantity or may be relevant to other organizations. It might or might not be valued by society. The lesser that is known about or more diverse the context in which the talent resides, the harder it is to identify talent, and the level of unrecognized talent increases.

Types of Talent

Different types of talent are relevant to the flow of talent depending on known or unknown perceived value and context.

- *Genius talent.* At the apex of known perceived value and context, Genius Talent is recognized as an extraordinary capability, which is difficult to reproduce. Even if the talent is not relevant to the achievement of the organizational strategic goals, it has a known perceived value and the context of its genius is known even if it is outside of the organizational context, for example, the contribution of Einstein to the field of physics, Mozart to music, or Mohammed Ali to sport.
- *Strategic talent.* Capability is what an organization highly values and has recognized as essential to the delivery of current strategic priorities. This talent is known within the current strategic context and regarded as essential to the delivery of the strategy and, as such, has a known perceived value. For example, Chambers et al. (1998) coined the term "The War for Talent" to highlight the known perceived value of good leadership skills regardless of organizational context.
- *Talent within.* Talent within is recognized within the known organizational context, but has reduced perceived value compared to strategic talent. This talent may have a low perceived value in

regard to contributing to strategic priorities or are lower down the organizational hierarchy, and so hold less intrinsic value, but may have some value operationally. This may result in individuals being recognized as high performers but not as having high potentials.

- *Expert talent.* Talent has a high, perceived value because of the recognition of the expert level of skill, knowledge, or ability possessed. The identification of expert talent is not necessarily within the organizational context, but does have intrinsic value in regard to a professional field relating to the activities of the organization. Its perceived value is likely to be higher within a professional context or in regard to recognition by a professional body. It is possible that Expert Talent might transition to strategic talent.
- *Candidate talent.* It is a recognized talent that has a high perceived value within the labor market and to the organization in regard to closing talent gaps that are hindering the achievement of strategic priorities. Candidate talent does not currently reside within the organization, but the organization will seek to attract the candidate talent as an applicant in the recruitment process.
- *Redundant talent.* This is recognized talent that is perceived to be of little value and is not required or is outdated. There may be considered to be an excess of this type of talent in the organization, resulting in a loose labor market, which reduces its perceived value. People with low-skill occupations or perceived as having no skill fall into this category. However, a talent not considered to be of value to society does not necessarily mean it has no value at all if it is adapted or developed. For example, consider the changing role and status of those with a talent in computer game development, with the introduction of gamification, online marketing, app development, and the growth in the gaming industry.
- *Unrecognized talent.* Talent that has not been identified because of a lack of self-awareness of the individual, inadequacy in the identification of talent by organizational processes, or shortcomings in society celebrating talent differences.

Talent and Job Roles

It is of course important that an organization ensures that everything that all the job tasks that need to be done are completed, and the Boundary-less Talent Management Model approach focuses on talent and strengths of the employees rather than job role. It is important to realize that just as some individuals cannot understand why anyone would want to spend time on writing detailed reports, or networking with complete strangers there will be other individuals who not only are good at doing these things but also *love* doing these things. On a practical level, the organization will need to manage the customization of job role. And one way of doing this is by segmenting employees into categories that share similar talents; in doing so, the organization can begin to cost-effectively manage the customization of job role. At first glance, the idea of an organization with thousands of employees individualizing job roles seems impossible. This is where organization design and structure can learn from the marketing profession, just as marketers have built mechanisms to target the consumer, an organization is able to construct segments of employee talent. Employees expect to be treated as an individual and because of this change organizations must learn how to customize the work environment and the job role to the individual talent within their organization

An alternative is to segment job activities into modules of activities that will enable the individual to select from a vast array of tasks, project, and activity choices based on what they do best. To help navigate the choices available, the organization may choose to invest in technology that could present individuals with only the most relevant tasks, project, and activity choices based on their talent, skills, and experience. This approach would also enable individuals to broaden their capability and build skill and experience in areas that they may not have the opportunity to develop when restricted by job description and traditional hierarchy.

The organization could also allow employees themselves to build work streams, projects, and programs in pursuit of organizational purpose and strategy. Instead of relying on a small team of colleagues, the individual employee may look up required talent, skills, knowledge, or experience using an internal organization version of LinkedIn. This would be the purest version of the network organizational structure.

Whatever route the organization chooses to build a job role based on what an individual does best, it is for the organization to encourage the individual to develop self-awareness of their talents and help them to take responsibility for growing, enhancing, and building it through learning opportunities.

Discovering the Talent Within

Often "talent" is equated with academic achievement. and academic achievement is perceived to equate to intelligence. This often means individuals who do not fit into the narrow confines of the education system feel written off, no good at anything, and downbeat about their potential because they don't have qualifications or were failed by the education system. Although steps are being taken to create opportunities for those who are vocational rather than academic, this route is still viewed as second class rather than an opportunity to develop talent; which is ironic, given the difficulty many organizations are having finding the engineering skills they require.

Helping an individual find and develop *their* talent within is as important as giving the talent within the organization room to roam in an organization. The first step for any organization is to debunk the myth about what *talent* means. Traditional talent management programs and processes talk of high potentials and are limited to the elite, future leaders in the organization. This narrow definition of talent is counterproductive. It creates division in the workforce of those who get invested in and developed and those who do all the hard graft. It also means that the organization loses out on all the untapped talent available to it.

Good organization design will ensure that talent identification is egalitarian. Talent can be anything, and it does not have to be grandiose or something that would put someone center stage but rather creates an environment for sustainable performance where talent can be identified, developed, and released.

Everyone in the organization will have talent, but in focuses on talent capacity required to achieve the organizational purpose it will become apparent that there are individuals whose talents aren't actually needed within the organization. These individuals need to be supported to move on, and it is not necessary for the organization to invest in talent that is not needed to achieve its purpose.

Providing systems to support individuals that enable the individual to explore and discover the things they *just do* or are *good at* is essential in the talent identification process. Very often, this uncovers activities that when individuals are asked to explain how they did something they can't give a coherent answer because they just *did it*. There is no conscious process and there are no coherent steps. An individual will discover a number of areas where they work with the talent within that *flows* within their ability. It is as natural to them as breathing. The individual is unconsciously *able* in their talent.

Part of identifying talent is for individuals to build self-awareness around what they just do and to begin a self-appreciation of the talent of doing things that come naturally and easily to them. In addition, conversations with their colleagues about what their colleague's value in them will also highlight areas of talent. Once talent has been identified, it is important that both the organization and the individual invest resource (time and money) to develop the talent within.

The Individual and Purpose

Just as an organization must have an expressed purpose, a reason to exist, so too must the individual within the workplace. Very often organizations expect individuals to leave their personal emotions, thoughts, and ideals at the door when they walk in. But, as discussed in Chapter One, purpose brings meaning to an individual's day-to-day work. An individual's values drive the way they interact with other people and with the work they do. If they are not allowed to express their purpose and their reason for existing in what they do in a day-to-day setting, they will be prevented from achieving their full potential. Being able to express their purpose has consequences for an individual in both their work and their life.

The Talent Within and Purpose

If individuals are unable to express their talent in their day-to-day work activity, organizational purpose cannot be sustained or achieved. It is the ability of employees to express their potential flowing into the purpose of the organization, which helps engender an environment for sustainable performance. Without talent, organization purpose cannot be expressed or achieved. With talent being released to achieve its full potential, the achievement of organizational purpose becomes possible. The talent within breathes life into organizational purpose and creates the pathways by which organizational activities have the momentum to move the organization forward.

The Talent Within and the Leader in Me

Getting the right type of leadership talent for the organizational purpose and also the team they are leading is essential for retention. A leader is only successful if they pay attention to both the talent of individual members in their team and how individuals are able to work together as a team. Leaders must make decisions about what organizational capacity is required to achieve the organizational purpose. Through selection, expectation setting, motivating, feedback, and developing their people, leaders of people will manage the talent within the organization. Leaders of expertise must also contribute by mentoring, supporting, and equipping individuals with the necessary knowledge and access to expertise to drive an individual's job performance.

The Talent Within and Harmonious Communities

The networked opportunity of working within a harmonious community provides additional opportunities for individuals to work with other people, utilize their talent, and develop their skills and knowledge. By working in cross-functional teams, it is possible for individuals to be exposed to expertise and learning that they may not in a siloed environment. Furthermore, it is possible for individuals to develop communities of practice with individuals who have similar talent, to learn from each other, share best practice, knowledge, and resources. Matrixed and project working enables individuals to tap into collective talent within the organization, resulting in increased innovation, creativity, and agility.

The Talent Within and Organizational Habitat

The dynamic and complex nature of the business environment means that careers are no longer based on a hierarchical ladder, but instead are characterized by inter-organization mobility. There gig economy and portfolio careers are upending traditional talent management processes and succession planning for organizations. The organization must regard the talent within as a resource that flows through the organization. With clarity about what capability is available, the organization is able to adapt and flex to changes in internal and external influences.

The Talent Within and Organizational Husbandry

Developing a plan to identify the strategic talent resource available to the organization internally and externally to the organization. This talent resource is an input into the organization's strategic plan, and therefore sustainable talent systems in regard to where the skills required to deliver the organization's strategic objective need to be secured in the same way as sustainable finance or other capital resources. This goes beyond traditional workforce planning, headcount, organization design, and identifying gaps, but rather becomes an iterative process of shaping the talent resource in response to changing strategic priorities.

The Talent Within and Creative Adaptation

When people do jobs that don't fit their talent, they struggle to be productive and can become very transactional in the work that they do. It sucks the soul out of people, unable to be everything they can be, individuals will retreat into doing tasks. The idea of self-actualization is not a new one and its value in releasing innovative thinking and creative capability is well documented and researched. If an organization is to benefit from the creativity that every single one of its employees possesses, then helping them to tap into the talent within is essential. In today's fast-moving, dynamic, and complex business environment, creative adaptation is the key ingredient to organizations being able to adapt, flex, and respond to the context and maintain competitive advantage. Utilizing every available talent within the organization will make that process more effective and efficient.

The Talent Within and Energy Transformation

Energy transformation requires an efficient utilization of organizational resources during the transformation process in order that organizational inputs can produce desirable outputs for the organization. The transformation process requires the organization to commit investment into the talent within (Input) in order to develop and enhance the talent capacity available to the organization. Like any other capital resource, it is imperative that organizational leaders take responsibility to make the best use of the resource available to it. Underinvestment in talent is like underinvestment in any other capital resource. Short term may have few consequences, but in the long term it can be catastrophic. It is also worth noting that developing the strengths of an individual has a far greater return on investment (Outputs) than investing in weaknesses.

The Talent Within and Organizational Cycling

Helping individuals to work in and with their talent is a sustainable people management practice, which enables the organization to improve levels of retention and higher levels of productivity than working against the talent within, which produces resistance and negative energy within the organization. However, it must also be recognized that the organization will need to work with the flow of talent through the organization. With flatter organizations, it is not possible to meet the growth and development needs of all employees; therefore, the organization must develop a culture of openness and honesty around career progression. A proactive exit strategy, coupled with developing a bench strength of potential candidate, will mean that the succession planning begins before an individual is an employee and after an individual stops being an employee.

Summary

- Developing people and discovering and releasing the talent within does not have to be expensive, but it does need attention.
- The importance of talent within the organization's design cannot be underestimated.
- The right people need to have the right capability for the organization they work for.
- Developing a clear and objective talent identification system is the foundation stone upon which the talent management process within the organization sits.
- Good organization design will ensure that talent identification is egalitarian.
- Talent is defined "as knowledge, skills or ability that an individual or organization perceives as recognizable capability that has intrinsic value."
- Determinants of talent are perception and context.
- Help individuals build self-awareness around what they just do and to begin a self-appreciation of the talent of doing things that come naturally and easily to them.

CHAPTER 5

Harmonious Communities

Collaboration is the connective tissue of organizations; it helps people to link their knowledge and expertise in a way that benefits the organization and its people

—John McGurk

The way we work has changed significantly in the past few decades due to political, economic, social, and technological change in the wider environment. The need for organizations to connect individuals together to work effectively within a harmonious community is essential if the organization is going to be able to deliver objectives. Collaboration is an essential component to enable individual employees to perform. Each employee is affected by, and affects those, people that they work with and alongside as part of their day-to-day work life. The structure of modern business and increased globalization present teams with additional challenges to successful and harmonious teamwork, including the navigation of flexible and remote working, managing operations across time zones, and managing individuals with different working and cultural practices. With the opportunities for collaboration enhanced by the increase in technology available, many organizations are not achieving their potential in regard to creating an online space in which virtual teams can collaborate with each other. Over 57 percent of IT managers believe that their organizations are not mining the potential of online collaborative tools. Diversity generally improves team working, but it does require team members to be more open-minded and focused on working together to find the best solution to problems that the organization is facing (Future Foundation, 2010).

The effectiveness of teamwork within the organization can be a positive or negative force within the business, as collaboration and cross-functional work is an essential part of organizational life. However, effective teamwork and the development of a harmonious community do not happen by accident. Organizational leaders must have a clear understanding of the nature of teams, how different organization structures and a number of challenging factors contribute to the opportunity for a team to be effective. The contribution of these elements need to be developed, coherently coordinated, and aligned in order that individual employees can be bought together in harmony so the organization community as a whole can respond to the competitive environment. Knowing who in the organization is as important as what you know about the organization, because it can support creative problem solving, ensure access to key information and can smooth the path for creative problem solving, and program implementation. Informal connections can very quickly form into formal project groups. Developing an internal web increases agency for organization activity and improves collaborative relationships between departments.

Alignment of the individual parts enables teams to deliver a more comprehensive, efficient, and effective response to organization challenges and opportunities much more than can be achieved when individuals operate alone. Combining team member skills, knowledge, and experience to deliver human cooperation adds value as the combination of group effort is far more valuable than the sum of the parts. In addition, individuals derive personal benefits from being part of an effective team, resulting in feelings of satisfaction and achievement. As the individual is elevated, the whole team experiences the benefit as a result of positive interaction, shared experience, shared endeavor, and the satisfaction of a team spirit. The net benefit results in increased levels of creativity, innovation, and a supportive and harmonious environment.

Components of a Harmonious Team

Collaboration is a key component of work within an organizational environment. The Decisive Decade Report, an international study by The Future Foundation (2010) for Google, reveals that there is an 81 percent correlation between collaboration and innovation. If organizations create an environment where their employees are actively supported in collaborating with each other, then they are 62 percent more likely to contribute new ideas to the organization (Future Foundation, 2010). Whether it is the reliance on someone else to provide information, complete their part of a process, or the combination of skill, knowledge, and experience to develop solutions to problems, working with others is a basic element of organizational life. Regardless of whether an employee is a senior or junior employee, work must be organized, usually based on role or task to achieve a common purpose. A team is a group of people, usually made up of four to six members, who are working together to achieve a common purpose. Although dysfunctional teams are common in many organizations, there are a number of factors that contribute to team and organization harmony.

Even working within a multinational enterprise with thousands of employees, a small team size will ensure that communication is effective and work is easily coordinated. Small team sizes ensure that team cohesion is supposed and reduces the occurrences for infighting and the development of factions. Each team member will be wedded together by sharing a common purpose (See Chapter One) and will interact to develop solutions to the same problems. Harmonious teams will have the responsibility for delivering a team objective for which they have collective accountability. This interdependency, coupled with a collaborative culture, helps individuals to take personal responsibility to get it right for the team and strive to deliver their work to a high standard, share information, and work to achieve success for each other. Developing a community membership, a sense of belonging and understanding that everyone is contributing to a bigger purpose will enable the development of high morale, individual and team motivation, and unite the team for the common purpose. Finally, driving a feeling of individual accountability within the community and driving willingness for individuals to be answerable for his or her actions and decisions will enable people to recognize how the choices they make have a power to contribute to the successful achievement of the purpose.

The Nature of Teams

For a harmonious community to become a reality, it is important that members of team collaborate with other teams so that the objectives of the organization can be achieved. The manager and team members will influence how effective the organizational community would be as a whole. Avoiding siloed working requires the sharing of information, knowledge, and best practice across the company and ensuring that people do not work in isolation. Planning workload is also essential, since poor planning can lead to issues with bottlenecks created by teams being unaware of work that is in the pipeline. Coordination and communication with agreed priorities will avoid missed deadlines. Making this a reality requires individuals to make time to share resources and focus on rewarding collaborative efforts rather than individual contribution. Rewarding employees for contributing to the creation of ideas also seem to be lagging behind the opportunity, with 58 percent of employees surveyed saying they would come up with more ideas if they were financially rewarded. Directly rewarding ideas generation in employees would help unlock the innovation possibilities available to the organization (Future Foundation, 2010). However, navigating the territory between harmonious working and groupthink where group members are pressured in maintaining harmony versus feeling safe to discuss their reservations and concerns about decisions being made is essential. Harmonious communities have space for challenge, questioning, and willingness to acknowledge differences.

Compatibility of values and shared purpose requires that organizational leaders regularly review the contribution of each individual and be honest and transparent about where gaps and problems exist. This also means careful selection of new members, considering the impact on the existing team members to ensure that productivity is maintained and enhanced. This goes beyond simply matching skills and experience and considers the personality of team members to ensure individuals complement each other.

Social Network Theory

Foster (2017c) explored social network theory by Katz et al. (2004: 308), who described a social network as "a set of actors ('nodes') and the relations ('ties' or 'edges') between these actors. The nodes may be individuals, groups, organizations or societies." In simple terms, a network is a set of relationships that are linked together. Social Network Theory (SNT) seeks to explain how and why people create, preserve, or discontinue ties, as well as explains the impact that networks have on an individual's behavior, attitude, opportunities, and constraints. The focus is on whether people form networks based on self-interest, collective need, reliance on others, or a mutual bond with like-minded individuals. There are three types of networks identified in theory:

- *Egocentric networks.* These are connected with a single node or relationship, such as good friends in firms that only do business with the organization and no one else.
- *Sociocentric networks.* These networks are networks within a closed boundary, for example, connections between colleagues in an office or participants in a workshop.
- *Open-system networks.* These networks have blurred boundaries and consist of connections that are not necessarily clear or obvious; they consist of chains of people or organizations.

The types of network will usually overlap with one another, and there will be relationships that extend along components of different systems within the web of the network.

So What?

The study of networks is concerned with why networks exist, why individuals choose to be connected and interact with other members of their network, how members interact, and how connected those members are. The researchers try to understand how a network works and offer an explanation as to why seemingly random people end up being connected. From the perspective of the harmonious community, SNT provides the basis for the examination of the quality of the network that is in place. An individual might have thousands of followers on Twitter, friends on Facebook, and links on LinkedIn, but this doesn't mean any interaction is taking place nor that the network has any value in regard to delivering a powerful information system, knowledge access, or influence.

Theory in Practice

The SNT can be used to understand how a harmonious community can support individuals and teams to develop connected relationships and access to knowledge and information, which can be a game changer in relation to problem solving.

- Empower individuals to focus on building a network as a regular activity. This should not be left to when individuals are working on a specific task. Help teams to make a habit of reaching out to people who are interesting by showing an interest in what they do.
- Avoid the tendency of network only being contacted when something is needed from them. The panhandler approach to networking is transactional and superficial and dries up the flow of a network very quickly. Encourage individuals to be a likable presence instead of a manipulative pain in the backside.
- Ensure that teams do their homework when connecting with someone. Networking should never be simply about collecting followers, rather it's about developing relationships, and that requires genuineness in making a connection, which requires mutual interest.
- Recognize people who are power contacts within the organization and external to it; these are individuals that have access either to other useful contacts for referrals or to information. Emphasize on keeping in touch with power contacts and make sure there is mutual support and exchange. This goes to the heart of the quality over quantity argument. Having the right people in the organizational network is more important than having numerous meaningless contacts.
- Cut out the networking parasites. Help support individuals to cut out those contacts who are only interested in directional relationships that draw from the organizational resources and gives nothing in return.
- Build on what you already have. Use relationship management software to update and review current networks and consider how the organization can increase its web of influence.

- Encourage individuals to follow up and keep in touch, responding professionally and politely to messages from the network. This may include the establishment of an alumni network.

Establishing Harmonious Communities

A number of factors contribute to establishing effective team working. These include:

- Establishing common goals supports cooperation on the basis of shared values and priorities.
- Defining roles and responsibilities helps to encourage group-centered behavior and promote individual satisfaction.
- Allocating work with the establishment of clear timelines for completing tasks provides clarity to the team and helps team functioning and focus on key priorities.
- Establishing clear reporting processes and lines of accountability enables team members to operate effectively regardless of organization structure.
- Developing mechanisms for both individual and team support will increase cohesiveness and promote information sharing, social interaction, and group identification.
- Maintaining focus on purpose and encouraging sharing information about team activity and celebrating progress and achievement will drive motivation.
- Providing access and encouraging the utilization of technology will enable effective communication between the team regardless of location and time zones.
- Respect is an essential component, especially in regard to treating others with consideration, to enable the creation of environment for sustainable performance.
- Changing the focus to be that of valuing the talents and contribution that others make in the team enables individuals to understand how they can support each other in achieving the organizational purpose.
- Honesty and integrity within the team environment is an important behavioral competency. Having the strength of mind and

courage to challenge each other constructively and yet remain supportive is essential if the team is to operate effectively.

• Having a common purpose that all members of the team can connect to gives meaning to the existence of the team. When there is disagreement and challenge within the team, providing a united front and agreed direction in communicating externally to others is nonnegotiable if the team is to have any credibility.

Fluidity of Teams

By tapping into the collective talent gathered from around the networked organization, it is possible to use group cohesion cross functionally to complete business-related tasks. A team or a third-party service provider may normally complete these tasks, but through collaboration the organizational community can assist in the completion of these tasks. It enables the expansion of an organization talent pool from pockets of performance to a sharing of expertise, knowledge, skill, and experience.

If employees are able to collaborate in the truest sense, the community as a whole responds to a needs-based process; they may not simply do what they are told, but are able to form cohesive groups that think differently about what is needed to help achieve the organization's purpose. Relationship building is an essential element of this process, and time must be given to ensure quality relationships can be developed.

In addition, collaboration does not need to be confined within the internal environment of the organization. The external network is a personal network owned and built by the individual. It is within the external network that the individual will develop their personal power and authority. It widens access to both information and resources. How the individual decides to develop their external network and how much effort they dedicate to building a network will determine how powerful the external networks are. Developing an external network provides access to information, knowledge, and influence.

Collaboration for skill, experience, and data resources can reach externally as well, making the boundaries of the organization more porous and allowing talent and skills to migrate in and out of the organization without restriction. This includes tapping into the professional networks that team members may be part of and inspiring individuals to tap into sources of expertise that they may have access to. All organizations have a wealth of knowledge, skill, and experience within their employee population, but the challenge is whether the required knowledge, skill, and experience are available when needed to support critical organizational initiatives. Finding and building strong collaborations with required resources can enable the organization to develop and perform in areas where it may otherwise not have the opportunity.

Involving the employee base in decision making and identifying areas where problems exist without obvious solutions will encourage individuals to volunteer their skills and knowledge to contribute to the decision-making process. Empower individuals based on their contribution rather than their hierarchical position. High-involvement strategies to enable team to develop self-managing work streams and develop task forces based on the skill sets of employees will build teams based on logical and prudent problem solving. Agility and flexibility in building connections, open communication, and applying processes whereby individuals can utilize their strengths and can be adopted into groups to help complete team tasks will provide the environment whereby the organizational community can respond to changing requirements. Good collaboration skills should be developed, including:

- The ability to work with others whether inside or outside the organization where improved value can be delivered.
- The sharing of information and insights, discouraging hoarding, or the building of knowledge fortresses.
- Regular communication of the overall purpose and keeping in mind the end goal.
- Allowing individuals to be creative in developing approaches to collaborative working and connecting with others.
- Paying attention to relationship building.

Managing the Performance of Teams

Achieving balance in organization design will be reliant on group collaboration. One of the key challenges of a performance management system will be measuring effectiveness of a group of individuals where the true measure of individual performance is their contribution to the performance of the team as a whole. This means it is often difficult to measure the performance of an individual, simply because the dynamics of working in a group environment means that their delivery objectives are reliant on other members of their group performing their job tasks equitably.

In this situation, the leaders in the business will need to clarify what it is that the organization is expecting of the individual to be contributing to the team performance and the relationship between the team performance and that of the individual's performance review. It will also be necessary to highlight how each expectation relates to succession planning and reward decisions.

Although measuring team performance is difficult because of the interdependence within the team on other people's contribution, this is an important area of performance management in the balanced organization. Where individuals are measured as a member of a team, there is an additional motivation to deal with any performance issues within the team dynamic, including conflict resolution and team management of individual performance. This behavior has been well documented in organizations that operate on the basis of self-managed teams, including Pret-a-Manager and Semler.

Harmonious Communities and Purpose

A common purpose is the glue that holds the team and the organization together. It provides the direction that the team have committed to travel and each individual must be supported to understand how he or she personally contributes to helping the organization achieve its purpose. In this way each team member will know why work needs to be done and what they need to, which in turn will help them to focus on the end goal.

Harmonious Communities and the Leader in Me

Effective team management relies on principle and personal accountability rather than just simple hard work and determination of the team members. Effectiveness can be linked to the approach that a manager takes to a given team and the management style employed. The leader of people must balance the needs of the individual with the needs of the team, and this requires that they understand what each individual needs to get from their work. In addition, the leader of people must ensure there is equity in the treatment of each member of the team, and that poor performance is dealt even-handedly. Staying impartial but committed to understanding and empathy, the leader of people is key to the development of a harmonious community.

Harmonious Communities and the Talent Within

A networked organizational habitat coupled with team community ethos will expand the boundaries of team beyond that of the immediate team role. In fact, the network itself will provide a huge opportunity for individuals to utilize and develop their talent. A harmonious community provides fertile ground for learning and experimentation within a safe environment. Relationship building and networked working will give individual exposure to different communities allowing them to develop a self-awareness of talent that they may not have understood they possessed. It also allows for different talent communities to combine, leading to a greater utilization of the collective talent within the organization.

Harmonious Communities and Organizational Habitat

Organization design for balance will require the organization to develop a networked structure to make it natural for networks and communities to evolve and remove barriers to collaboration. Individuals and teams will become empowered to complete management tasks at team and individual levels, which feed into further development of the harmonious community structure. Leaders will either provide a supportive role for people or proactively support the management of knowledge and transfer of expertise across the organization.

Harmonious Communities and Organizational Husbandry

Communities need to be self-sustaining, and well-developed processes will facilitate and positively contribute to the development of teams and growth of positive team dynamics. Ensuring there is a focus on the community aspect while giving space and time for relationships to develop will result in strong bonds and personal investment in what the organization is trying to achieve and in sustaining the community itself. To make this a reality, there needs to be a continuous recognition that support is available, and more important processes and systems are provided to manage cross-functional working. A continuous celebration of diversity and support processes that deliver interconnectivity and allow communities to evolve naturally rather than being confined by an unnatural best-practice construct that has no bearing on the work or reality of the community in question.

Harmonious Communities and Creative Adaptation

Communities of practice should be hubs of innovation as the collective talent available to the organization builds on ideas from individual employees. Reward practices should be focused on rewarding individuals for contributing to the collective and outcomes rather than focusing on the singular contribution of the individual. Performance focused on contributing the collective and doing what is right for the community will allow more complex innovation and creativity to emerge.

Harmonious Communities and Energy Transformation

Organizational leaders must check on how effective teams are working, and if and where there are issues, ensure that they are not ignored. Leaders of people should be on hand to provide support, which may be in the form of a team intervention, individual coaching, or skills developed if needed. There should be no room for fear of managing individuals who are problematic but instead ingroup/outgroup dynamics should be tackled head on. As far as possible, efforts should be made to link being ingroup to the alignment of the individual and team with the purpose of the organization and outgroup behaviors to those who are not going in the same direction and are acting against the development of community. This is not the same as those who challenge or raise concerns about what is being done—rather the manner in which challenge is given: transparent and open versus subversive and marginalizing people. Support should also be given to those who have outgrown the organization's mission, so that right up to the last day of work individuals feel they can work for the good of the community rather than in opposition. Finally, accountability for personal impact and collective responsibility for team impact should be imperative for everyone, regardless of time served or seniority.

Harmonious Communities and Organizational Cycling

It is part of human nature to seek out community and develop relationships, but disharmony does happen too, and this should be acknowledged as part of the natural cycle of human endeavor. Sustainability can only be achieved if everyone is invested in creating a community where relationships matters—and relationships cannot be exclusive or excluding. Leaders of people needed to wield their considerable talent at bringing people together, managing people who are suffering from personal issues, and developing cohesion between and within teams. Where community is broken, it must not be allowed to fester. Intervention is essential to ensure any disharmony does not become contagious.

Summary

- Effective teamwork and the development of a harmonious community do not happen by accident.
- Well-built harmonious communities offer the organization a powerful information and knowledge system that gives access to private sources of information, access to people, a source of influence and authority, and the opportunity to acquire competence.
- Informal connections can very quickly form into formal project groups.
- Developing an internal web increases agency for organization activity and improves collaborative relationships between departments.
- In simple terms, a network is a set of relationships that are linked together.
- From the perspective of the organization, SNT provides the basis for the examination of the quality of the network that is in place.

CHAPTER 6

Organizational Habitat

The information age has ushered in a networked and interdependent world, one in which challenges and opportunities appear and disappear faster than traditional organizational models can manage.
—Chris Fussell

If organizational balance is similar to an ecosystem, then organizational habitat is the environment that is created in which organizational activity can take place. Traditional organizational design approaches set strategy and design around the strategy. The organizational habitat proposes a different approach to designing organizational architecture. In the digital economy there needs to be flexibility and agility in organizational structure, which traditional hierarchical organizations struggle to accommodate. Creating a networked internal architecture within the organization, managing the network for flexibility and agility, and utilizing the network to adapt effectively to change and respond to challenges from both the internal and external environment requires a "land-management-based approach."

What this means in regard to organizational design is to approach the organizational architectural environment like a farmer or landowner. Working with the land, rather than working against it—understanding the soil, the environmental conditions, and those who occupy the land. Globalization has changed the business environment and the workplace considerably. Organizations with hierarchical architecture may still exist, but the traditional structures that accompany them are no longer fit for purpose. Flatter organizational structures and cross-functional working, sometimes across multiple geographic locations, help organizations to adapt and flex to the contextual demands. Hierarchy and top-down approaches to managing organizations worked when organizations could be sure of mechanical processes and foundations; but in an era of globalization and tremendous change and flux, this structure is no longer sustainable in the long term—except with regular restructures that are time-consuming, disruptive, and costly.

In regard to people management, the traditional command and control, rules and required behaviors that are driven by a hierarchical structure prevent individuals from releasing the talent within and working collaboratively. The experience of individual employees, many growing up with the Internet, Twitter, and Facebook is of open lines of communication and open exchanges of opinion. In a world where we can email the prime minister, instantly express our opinion on a discussion posted by the president of the United States on Twitter, or befriend everyone from our next-door neighbor to our favorite bands and celebrities, decisions being made by a select few behind closed doors are no longer culturally acceptable.

Organizational Habitat

Organizational habitat refers to the organizational structures, processes, systems, and practices that create an organizational environment capable of creating sustainable performance.

The way business is conducted has changed as a result of a highly competitive marketplace and because of the digitalization of the workplace. Organizations, through a process of delayering, have become flatter but the majority is still hierarchical. This has an impact on the environment in which employees work. Processes and systems are designed to maintain a hierarchy and pecking order, not just in terms of who signs off what, who has access to what, but also in regard to the flow of information throughout the organization. Politics and politicking are a common problem in organizational life, what you know, who you know, and how you play the game become more important than ensuring that the workplace is healthy, effective, and delivering an environment where everyone thrives. It becomes about winners and losers, scaling the ladder, personal agendas, and developing siloed fiefdoms. The Peter Principle (Peter, 1969) highlights how an individual's performance in their current role is the basis of progression, but performance in the current role can also hide an individual's failings or true talent, if they are in the wrong role. Spending time identifying the talent within is part of the solution, but creating an even playing field is also a mechanism whereby those who work against the organization will be weeded out. Moving away from a traditional pyramid-shaped organization architecture, no matter how flat the hierarchy toward matrix working will result in less formal structures and lead to cross-functional and multidisciplinary working. This is turn leads to a cross-fertilization of ideas and contributes to creative adaptation within the organization. However, as with all structural designs, development of harmonious communities is a key ingredient. An enforced matrix structure can contribute to reduced team performance, which is a barrier to the development of group dynamics, and team behavior are ignored. Individuals need familiarity and if you have a team that works well together, forcing them to work on other projects could be disastrous to productivity. A fine balance therefore needs to be developed between flexibility and matrix working and static hierarchy that prevents cross team working. Confronting issues that impact on effective team working are important if the organizational habitat is going to develop into a place that nurtures individuals, delivers harmonious communities, and delivers organizational purpose.

Developing a Network of Flexibility and Support

The structure and design of an organization needs to be able to cope with changes to the environment while still providing stability to manage the organizational activities. There needs to be flexibility, agility, and support design into the structure.

The design of an organization's habitat is the result of a number of choices and decisions based on what is required in order to achieve an organization's purpose. The right organizational habitat will increase the opportunity for sustainable performance and the organizational purpose being achieved.

An organizational habitat needs to take into account the organizational capability such as:

- The talent within the organization that cannot be replicated by other organizations;
- Capabilities that have been developed internally by the organization;
- The progress of the organizational community toward harmony;
- Leadership capability and mix of leaders of people and leaders of expertise required to deliver organizational purpose; and
- Organizational factors that provide competitive advantage.

The answer is a network approach to organizational design. There may be centers of expertise or activity, but they interlink with other areas of business. These links can be changed easily and swiftly. The network is a fairly flat structure. Although there may be some thin layers, links can be made easily between levels.

The network structure requires that organizations, leaders, and employees to fundamentally rethink the way in which work gets done. Tasks, processes, and responsibility moves to a cross-functional team who are given the time and resources to accomplish their part in the organizational purpose. Individuals will probably work with more than one leader, very often being temporarily assigned to a project team. This may require the individual to manage the demands of several projects at one time, as their "day job" actually becomes a process of using their skills where they are required within the organization. Reporting lines therefore need to be flexible, communication transparent, and decision making will need to track across both horizontal and vertical team structures.

Managing in a Networked Organizational Habitat

In hierarchical organizational structures, the management structure will determine reporting lines with authority passed down the organization through a series of management levels. Line managers at the lower levels of hierarchy will be given responsibility for work that is task focused, whereas, further up the hierarchy, managers will be involved in decision making and delegation. The networked organizational habitat pushes power to the point of need. Fewer levels of management are required; senior leaders of expertise will be involved in the day-to-day tasks that they can contribute to based upon their individual talent and expertise. Leaders of people will become more senior based on the number of teams rather than individuals that they are supporting, but their day job remains the same: aligning people to purpose and ensuring that everyone is able to work effectively. The difference is that their focus is totally on the task of people management, not trying to fit people management around their management tasks. However, the management of tasks will be the responsibility of individuals and teams, who, through the network, will develop an understanding of what needs to be done to achieve the organization's purpose. The networked habitat is a fluid system with processes that allow people to respond to the needs of the organization rather than developing rigid structures that get in the way of getting things done. In the networked structure, both formal and informal groups are able to contribute to the commercial success of the organization. Even social interactions can bolster innovation and creativity, and group interactivity will provide the foundation of cooperative working to ensure tasks are completed and the organizational purpose is achieved. Contractors and specialists from outside the organization will also affect the effectiveness of the organizational structure. Understanding that boundaries of the organization don't stop with some artificial decision of who is or is not an employee. If specialist skills or expertise is required for particular tasks and projects, then anyone who can contribute to the purpose of the organization positively can become part of the group. However, support will need to be given to help groups going through dynamic inflows and outflows of talent to adapt and reestablish group norms and achieve high levels of performance.

The Virtual Habitat

Information technology has enabled the creation of the networked organization, in regard to both the development of an organizational environment in offices and the creation of the virtual organization, which exists in a digital environment. In this way, remote teams and harmonious communities are able to collaborate and work in real time via the cloud, file sharing, and online meetings. These online systems create a virtual habitat that will enable group communication and decision making. The benefits of such an organization are obvious. Time and location are removed as barriers to communities working together. However, the leadership of remote teams can be hugely challenging and must be managed with care. In today's hostile online environment, individuals, teams, and organizations as a whole must develop systems and processes that protect the security of information exchange. In addition, when working across the globe, with individuals operating across different time zones, timeliness of communication can cause issues with team effectiveness. E-communication also makes it more difficult to develop relationships based on trust and interpersonal communication. This can result in issues regarding cohesiveness and increase the possibility of detachment separation from team goals. Extra time and resource must be given to ensure those working virtually are able to develop and maintain healthy working relationships.

Practices to Support a Networked Organizational Habitat

There are number of organizational practices that can support a networked organizational habitat. These include:

- *Flexible working.* Flexible working includes allow employees to have flexible start and finish times, offering different shift patterns, and working in locations other than a central head office, for example, from home. Effective flexible working needs to balance the needs of the employee with the requirements of the organization for it to be effective.
- *Transferable skills.* Networked working and communities of practice require that employees develop transferable skills in addition to specific expertise, such as communication skills. This will allow individuals and teams to migrate where their talent is needed in response to the needs of the organization.
- *Contribution-based reward.* Reward practices need to focus on supporting teams based on the belief that the performance outcomes

of a network of individuals working together is greater than the sum of an individual's singular contribution.

- *Project/temporary teams.* The networked organizational habitat is predominately based on groups of individuals who will come together within the organization for either the delivery of a specific project or an interim period in order to achieve a particular task or deliverable outcome. Individuals will join and leave teams according to whether there is a need for their talent.

- *Remote teams.* Remote teams are required in multinational enterprises (MNEs), which will mean that team members will possibly be located in different geographic regions. Their ability to work across borders as a team relies on continual improvements in communication technology.

- *Diversity.* The networked organizational habituated requires all participants to embrace diversity and be adept at accommodating differing cultural and work practices. Some of this may be physical space within the organizational environment, for example, incorporating prayer rooms in office buildings, whereas other accommodations will be behaviorial and relies on cultural awareness.

- *Consensus decision making.* Everyone working within a networked organization habitat must seek out solutions, which everyone in the team can actively get behind and buy into. This is a more dynamic approach than the majority-rules approach most often taken in decision making and instead relies on everyone agreeing to a way forward.

- *People leadership.* A key aspect of the role of a leader lies in people acknowledging that relationships and people are at the center of their leadership practice will facilitate the creation of a supportive work environment to deliver results.

- *Mutual participation.* Information silos are destroyed, through either communication networks or knowledge management systems. In this way, information sharing and coordination by all stakeholders in a decision-making process becomes possible, and the focus on fostering cooperation results from mutual participation between different groups.

- *Multidisciplinary skills.* Due to the fast-paced competitive environment that most organizations operate in, coordination is required to ensure that teams are agile. Multidisciplinary teams are at the center of a networked structure and each individual should be respected for what they are able to contribute in regard to their range of skills and experience. Innovative solutions will be driven as a result of contributions from a number of different disparate professional fields.

Benefits of a Networked Organizational Design

The main benefit of a networked organizational structure is that it allows the flexibility and adaptability that is required for an organization to manage the balance it needs to create the environment for sustainable performance. Although breaking down traditional hierarchy and centers of power could be problematic, the networked structure will allow individual employees and leaders to focus resources on customer needs and improve competitive advantage. There are many commercial benefits, which can be attributed to networked organizational designs. Wickens (1995) stated that the strength of an organization is in its people, declaring that if an organization values its people, people will bring the organization value. When networking between people is part of the organizational culture, individuals will have a set of shared values, a strong sense of purpose that is clearly communicated to and grasped by employees. Furthermore, participation in decision making will result in high levels of productivity, profitability, and utilization of the strength of individuals and teams.

The network will also allow the organization to achieve synergy and leverage the talent in a timely manner, enabling the organization to exploit possible opportunities when they arise. From an individual employee's perspective, the networked structure will increase the opportunity for individuals to build and develop their strengths and competencies, increase expertise, and realize the potential of talent within the organization as a whole.

The difficulties of such a structure are around control. But here is where having leaders of people comes into its own. Just like servers in an IT network, leaders of people provide the link to other leaders and functions and mesh the organizational network together. The leader will often provide essential services across a network, either to employees inside the organization or to customers, suppliers, and shareholders. It will be the leaders who will facilitate the definition of the performance objectives of new groupings and ensure that they stay on track while providing them with the resources needed to achieve what is required.

The networked structure is an output of high involvement and empowerment among employees. To support such decentralization, information flows must be open and the perspective of career advancement shifts from an upward trajectory to recognition and celebration of talent. The network enables regular job rotation and the opportunity for individuals to take part in challenging assignments, giving them the visibility and experience need to advance. The structure removes the traditional career ladder and instead replaces it with different pathways, which are more in tune with the global economy as a whole. Greater levels of responsiveness and flexibility will lead to increased levels of group loyalty, which supports the organization as it seeks to find a positive response to external competitive pressures and changes in the market place. Katzenbach and Smith (1993) noted that shared commitment from groups results in a powerful unit of collective performance, helping teams to achieve specific performance goals.

One further advantage of the networked structure is the distribution of knowledge throughout the organization. Knowledge has huge value in the modern economy; but in traditional organizational structures, getting the required knowledge from one part of the organization to where it is needed is often complex. The network structure creates the mechanism for employees to gain access to the knowledge they need to complete their assignments and promotes knowledge transfer by encouraging sharing of knowledge not just internally but also externally. Developing the people resource and getting people together in open forums to work on solving problems can result in higher levels of efficiency. Increased responsiveness and flexibility is achieved by contributing, leading to a cycle of continuous improvement and harnessing work tasks on improving the energy transformation of the enterprise. Performance challenges coupled with collaborative decision making are a result of individuals being provided with opportunities by other members of the team to make a distinctive contribution. Therefore, it could be argued that networked working contributes to higher levels of individual performance, collaborative working, and consequently improved organizational performance.

The significance of personal relationships as recognized by Maslow (1970) is captured in the idea of self-actualization, which results in human fulfillment and well-being. The result of which is to improve levels of retention and reduced absenteeism. This in turn has the dual benefit of reducing costs of the organization and increasing engagement among employees that contributes to greater levels of innovation, thus resulting in improved revenue.

Organizational Habitat and Purpose

The organization habitat is an enabler of purpose. The establishment of a network and the removal of barriers will challenge individuals to work toward and align to the purpose of the organization. It will mean that teams and individuals will have to ask whether their planned endeavors are helping to deliver the purpose of the organization, and if it is not, individuals and teams are able to redeploy their talents on efforts which are helping to deliver.

Organizational Habitat and the Leader in Me

The organization requires that someone will protect the habitat in the same way that a gardener maintains a garden and ensures that every plant thrives, removes anything that threats the garden, and applies what is needed to cultivate the garden so that it thrives. Leaders of people are essential to the creation of a people-centered, networked organizational habitat. They will be responsible for ensuring that teams are established, roles clarified, and network connections supported. They will cultivate mutual trust between different parts of the organization, provide support to teams and individuals who may be struggling, and confront any group of individuals that is threatening the effectiveness of the team. Leaders of expertise also have a responsibility to enable the flow of knowledge through the organization, providing irrigation through the careful deployment of expertise and skill in the right place and at the right time.

They will also need to mentor individuals to help develop talent and ensure that knowledge is managed within the organization habitat.

Organizational Habitat and the Talent Within

A networked organization habitat can be designed to ensure that individuals are fully able to utilize their talent and that the organization can ensure that it has the right talent available in the right place at the right time. Individuals will experience the opportunity to fully realize their talent potential and the organization will benefit from high levels of utilization of the talent within. On a personal level, this will mean that individuals will be able to experience what it feels like to contribute to the achievement of purpose using their talent what it is needed. They will also be exposed to opportunities to develop their self-awareness through working within groups where other talents are being used. This in turn will broaden the experience and knowledge sharing within and across organizational boundaries and ensure that everyone benefits from continuous organizational learning.

Organizational Habitat and Harmonious Communities

Traditional organizational structures limit the opportunities for dynamic harmonious communities to be effective. Although formal teams may still form part of the organizational habitat, informal teams and project working will ensure that talent specialisms and shared ideas can cross functions easily. This can have a powerful effect on both the organization and group members. Communities of practice can draw in expert knowledge and skills to deliver a dynamic and effective approach to team problems, while individuals can fully utilize their skills and talents alongside like-minded people.

Organizational Habitat and Organizational Husbandry

A networked organizational habitat ensures that resources are where they need to be, when they are needed. Although management tasks are delegated across the organization and employees are empowered to make decisions, accountability and responsibility will ensure that resources are used for the good of the organization as opposed to individual pet projects. The networked organizational structure also enables the organization to flex and connect across the globe with ease.

Organizational Habitat and Creative Adaptation

Removal of artificial barriers will provide space for individuals and teams to develop solutions to problems in real time and quickly form response teams to issues arising from both internal and external environment. High levels of trust, respect, and empowerment will allow daring ideas to be explored and refined to ensure that solutions create value through creative ideation and adaptation.

Organizational Habitat and Energy Transformation

The organizational habitat ensures that the transformation process within the organization is smooth and can flow uninterrupted by artificial barriers and dams, which prevent inputs from being successfully converted into outputs. If something isn't working, it isn't tied to a hard structure that costs money to fix, instead the dynamism of the networked architecture allows functions, teams, and departments to be dissolved or established through consensus and team working. Projects can be set up swiftly with expertise drafted in as and when it is needed, failure cannot be hidden from view in silos where silence is encouraged to protect reputations. Instead, individuals are able to utilize their talents, learn from each other, learn from failure, and progressively adapt to changes within the organization.

Organizational Habitat and Organizational Cycling

Scanning for environmental changes is much easier when everyone within the organization is responsible for bringing pertinent information to the table. Those people who know what is working or not working are usually those people closest to the customer. Removal of hierarchy will mean that messages of change happening has little distance to travel and will not be lost in translation. It is the difference between looking through opaque glass with someone describing what is happening and being able to walk freely examining what is happening for yourself. Changes can be examined from different angles to ensure that the perspective that is being presented is as rounded as possible. Personal interests can be set aside as participatory decision making means that decisions made are those that are best for the organization in the long term. Inputs to the transformation process can be examined from the perspective of delivering what is needed not only for short-term survival but also for long-term sustainability without the fear of being overruled by people who know nothing of the particulars but have their own agendas.

Summary

- Organizational habitat refers to the organizational structures, processes, systems, and practices that create an organizational environment capable of creating sustainable performance.
- The structure and design of an organization needs to be able to cope with changes to the environment while still providing stability to manage the organizational activities.
- The network structure requires that organizations, leaders, and employees to fundamentally rethink the way in which work gets done.
- Tasks, processes, and responsibility moves to a cross-functional team who are given the time and resources to accomplish their part in the organizational purpose
- Reporting lines need to be flexible, communication transparent, and decision making will need to track across both horizontal and vertical team structures.
- Technology has enabled remote teams and harmonious communities to collaborate and work in real time via the cloud, file sharing, and online meetings.
- There are a number of organizational practices that can support a networked organizational habitat.
- There are many commercial benefits that can be attributed to networked organizational design.

CHAPTER 7

Organizational Husbandry

Never be afraid to try something new. Remember, amateurs built the ark; professionals built the Titanic.

—Anon

Organizational husbandry considers the moral duties that organizations have toward stakeholders and the wider society. Ethics and values are indelibly entwined with the idea of morality, or rather whether the operation and behavior of the organization, its leaders and employees are good or bad. Morals regulate the behavior of an individual or organization in a social setting and construct the framework of what behavior is necessary and acceptable in order to provide the opportunity for social harmony. Ethics and values are very often linked to philosophical thinking and the decisions we make as individuals and as a society as to what we believe constitutes right and wrong and what is good or bad. The philosophical questioning arises because what is good for one person may result in bad consequences for someone else. The problem with ethics and values is that each individual will have their own opinion as to what is right or wrong. Organization husbandry doesn't seek to avoid these dilemmas but instead encourages questions regarding the operation of the organization and taking steps to find a resolution. Morals, therefore, are an opportunity to provide a code of practice regarding the ethics and values that are important for the social and environmental balance that the organization is looking to achieve.

Organization's operates in a social context and every organization has the responsibility for delivering sustainable processes and practices, which considers how the cost of such processes and practices to both society and the environment is balanced with what is being given in return. Both the internal and external costs become part of the same balance sheet. For organizations, the calculation is whether the balance between business needs and sustainability delivers a return on investment, which justifies a particular action. The purpose is to develop confidence in knowing that what sustainable policies and practices the organization adopts to help others will lead not only to betterment of society and the environment but of business performance too.

If mistakes are made and bad things happen in the pursuit of profit, it will be morality and the accompanying ethics and values policies that will provide the map as to whether the organization or an individual deserves punishment or support. It is true that bad things do happen in business. Our action does not always align with the intention with which we set out. "I didn't mean that to happen" is not just an excuse, but is a common reaction where action has resulted in something that was not intended. This of course does not excuse recklessness or negligence when evaluating organizational husbandry. It will be the moral compass that will guide the judgment where things have gone wrong.

Organizational Husbandry
(Using What You Have Sensitively)

Organization husbandry explores sustainable organizational processes and practices and the development of a methodology and methods for using organizational resources sensitively. When the agenda changes to considering how to use what you have sensitively, there is a shift in the method by which judgment and decision is made. Pursuing a course of appreciative inquiry in decision making changes the atmosphere from one that is discriminatory and negative to one that focuses on what is sustainable as well as what is profitable. The key to organizational husbandry is that it is people-centered and therefore its core value is that people are valuable and have value beyond something that can be measured purely financially and that the organization has a social agenda in addition to an economic agenda. It is operating a business where kindness is not random and not unusual but part of the organization's raison d'etre and benefits not just those on the fringes of society who are in desperate need of kindness in order to live, but also those who have plenty but live in fear of having nothing.

Organization husbandry doesn't reject the need to grow an organization or deliver a healthy return on investment, instead it seeks to harness the human capability to be creative, inventive, and adaptable and adjust the attitude toward wealth creation as not being a win–lose equation but about achieving a win for all stakeholders. In doing so, there is a core value in organization balance that states that *people are valuable and have value.*

Profit is not presented as a bad or evil thing, but it should be pursued in the context of what profit will be used for, not as an end in itself. The profit agenda, social contribution, ethics, and values are back on the agenda as demonstrated by the examination of executive pay, tax avoidance by transnational organizations and the rejection of the Paris climate agreement by the Trump administration. Discussions about a more moderate and responsible form of capitalism and environment-friendly business practices are no longer the preserve of the Marxist agitators and are a regular part of boardroom discussions.

Organizational balance is born out of the need to interact sensitively with the internal and external environment in which the organization operates. Ignoring the impact of the natural environment and resources that interacts with organizational balance would be to ignore the truth of global climate change and the growing reality that in the near future businesses will be facing significant issues surrounding energy, water supplies, and even food supply. Organizations cannot ignore the challenges that planet earth is facing and continue operating in a manner that does not use natural resources sensitively and sustainably. In addition, the organization is part of a global system; its performance environment will be impacted by the increasing interconnectivity between global economies, corporations, and society as a whole. This means that organizations must understand that the ultimate consequences of any decision they make are at best poorly understood and at worst catastrophic to sustainable performance of the organization.

Organization Husbandry and Performance

Organization husbandry does not mean the organization will end up with a negative balance sheet. Sensitively using the resources of the organization adds something, not only to the group or individual who is on the receiving end, but also to the organization who is giving it. There have been numerous studies that demonstrate that sustainability is good for business. In November 2011, a "researcher from the Harvard Business School and London Business School published *The impact of a Corporate Culture of Sustainability on Corporate Behavior and Performance.* This study tracked the financial performance of matched pairs of companies over an 18-year period. Ninety 'high sustainability' companies, which had adopted a significant range of environmental and social policies since the early 1990s, were paired for comparison with 90 companies that were similar except for adopting few sustainability-orientated policies. The results showed that a £1 investment in a value-weighted portfolio of high sustainability firms in 1993 would have increased to £22.60 by the end of 2010, compared with a return of £15.40 from the low-sustainability performances. The high sustainability firms also significantly outperformed on other measures, including return on assets and return on equity." (CIPD, 2011) Organization husbandry doesn't mean adding cost to a business that impacts profit to such a degree that shareholders will not want to invest in the organization. But it does demand a change in mindset that requires a long-term investment lens rather than one that insists on fast return on investment at the expense not only of society at large, but also the long-term performance that the organization can deliver.

A community-based approach, focused on shared responsibility and delivering a sustainability agenda, will have other benefits; a sense of belonging, of being part of something bigger delivers huge benefits in regard to personal well-being and happiness. In addition, those with community ties are healthier, better nourished, and more able and willing to contribute to the social paradigm. Being part of something bigger makes us act bigger. It helps us to be better as well as feel better. Globalization of the world economy has reduced the size of the world, not just in regard to our ability to communicate and trade with other nations, but also in regard to our expectations and beliefs on what we can be achieve. It cements a belief that one organization can make a difference and can be a paragon of the triumph of the human spirit over adversity.

Stewards of Planet Earth

The environment and ecology of the planet earth is necessary for the provision of specific factors such as breathable air, habitable conditions, and the ability to sustain life, which are necessary for humanity to survive and flourish. The interaction between the environment, society, and technological aspects of our endeavors is essential in understanding the organization husbandry in the context of humanity as Stewards of Planet Earth. Organization balance promotes ethics, values, and moral choice, which support and promote harmony between humanity and the natural environment.

Human ingenuity has created technology, which has allowed us to harness natural resources and turned them into assets that are of significant value to our society. But a lack of regulation and competition for scarce resources has meant that we are creating a natural disaster of global proportions. Hostility toward regulation is endemic and failures that have been experienced in the financial market should serve as a warning of the potential problems that are being created in the environment because of a lack of robustness in regulating ownership and the use of natural resources.

There appears to be a misaligned faith in our ability to develop innovative technology, which will solve the problems with carbon emissions and other green house gases. But technology alone will not solve the problem of excessive reliance on fossil fuels, nor will it help organizations to be less wasteful. Instead, like a person embarking on a journey to lose weight, there must be a change in attitude and behavior toward consumption and waste if organizations are to become part of the change rather than expecting change to happen without organizational input.

Over the past decade, there has been a greater degree of challenge as to the rightness of industrialization without recourse to questioning our responsibility to support organized and active participation in environmental stewardship. Too often, we engage in large-scale industrial projects to manufacture products that will solve societal or political issues, with little consideration to the environmental impact of such technology, or indeed the subsequent cost of human activity on the wider environment;

not least the sustainability of plant and animal life. The pursuit of profit through driving consumption and materialism as well as the pursuit of growth at all costs has come into conflict with the need to preserve and conserve natural resources.

Prosperity and harmony with nature is possible, but we have yet to learn how to achieve one without failing at the other. Organizations fail to take responsibility for the external costs of their actions and yet there needs to be a determined effort to restore the balance between man and the environment.

Planetary and Organizational Assets

The argument between environmentalists and economists over the issue of who has ownership of natural assets is a complex one. When someone creates something themselves it appears fair that they should own that which they have created, but difficulty occurs when examining an asset that is essentially free to those who come across it. Whether it is precious minerals, oil, water, or land, the assets that planet earth endows upon humanity for use cannot be claimed to be property of anyone and whether they should be used for our consumption today or saved for the use of future generations, the questions of stewardship regarding natural assets isn't an easy one to resolve.

For assets such as oil that deplete and cannot be replaced, saving them for future generations cannot be defended immemorial; at some point, they will be used up and the asset will be gone forever. The onus on the generation using the depleted asset is to make sure that it is not wasted and that the most beneficial use is made from it while it remains.

How these planetary resources are used, however, must be considered in the wider context than simply private enterprise. The current situation means that the oligarchs maintain possession of such resources, at the cost to the wider society in the pursuit of private gain. Such possession has little to do with creativity, innovation, or development but rather as a result of luck, either as an accident of birth or being in the right place at the right time. Where assets can be renewed and replenished, such as fish stocks or agricultural land, the onus is on the current owners to ensure that its stewardship leaves the asset in at the least the same place, if not a better place than when it took possession of it. In this respect the environmentalists win the argument over the economists, at least in an ethical sense. We cannot allow the pursuit of profit to decide whether fishing the oceans and the extinction of fish species happens and especially when such a resource is part of our global food resource. Abuse and profiteering at the expense of a resource that, with continued mismanagement, cannot be recreated or fixed by a later generation if destroyed, requires organization husbandry. The question that organizations face therefore is how much growth is enough when balanced with protecting scarce natural resources.

Nature is different from the things that man builds for himself; it is part of a symbiotic relationship, which requires mutuality and careful attention. Nature as an asset is different for our normal understanding of assets, in a similar way that humans as a resource differ from other forms of capital resources. It is right that they are used to help us progress, but as we progress so too should we seek to enhance the well-being of the asset being used. The environment is not a static display in a museum that must be preserved as it is, but rather it has a dynamism that can be used to enhance the lives of humanity. We must accept the obligations of stewardship, delivering a management agenda based on ethics and values and a planned use of natural resources, which ensures that their full potential is used in the betterment of humanity.

Quite possibly we have reached a crossroads where humanity has finally discovered a convergence between industrialization, technology, and environmental awareness, which has created a dawning realization that we can no longer continue the way that we always have. Humanity is at an environmental crunch point where our continued pursuit of industrialization and abuse of natural resources have become unsustainable. We may yet avoid environment collapse, but research suggests that our use of natural resources, even those that are renewable, is exacting a too high a cost on the ecosystem and the result will be greater levels of disruption to civil society than we have yet experienced. Organizations are therefore faced with a choice where they must choose between economic actions that are destroying the environment or harnessing the productive capabilities, innovation, and inventiveness of the human entrepreneurial spirit for the protection of the wider environment and nature.

Organizations must have responsibility for and demonstrate a commitment to environmental stewardship and citizenship that respects "nature, universal rights, economic justice and a culture of peace." And those organizations imbued their purpose with a "responsibility to one another, to the greater community of life and to future generations" (Mayer, 2007). We must accept that we do not have true ownership of the natural resources, but, rather, that we are loaned them for a period of time and must ensure that we return them for future generations in the same, if not better, condition than they were given to us. Although planet earth cannot be treated as a museum, we must not allow it to become a mausoleum either. Preserving natural treasures, for continual use in the future is good stewardship of resources, which even the most utilitarian economist can appreciate.

Organization husbandry has to be seen in a holistic framework and solutions cannot be taken in isolation. Understanding the wider system within which the solution is operating can help those making the decision be aware of possible unintended consequences a decision made today may have on future generations. It is difficult for contemporary society to care too much for future generations and a population that have yet to live, especially when we have pressing concerns of our own, but all people, past, present, and future, are equal and the welfare of future generations must be taken into consideration and safeguarded as much as the contemporary populations' current needs and wants.

Husbandry of Talent

Another area of curiosity is in regard to the natural assets, or talents that we possess as individuals. We are all born with talent, or rather with possibility of what we can be if effort was applied in the right areas. Since it is part of who we are, our genetic makeup, our talent is in some respects a resource. Since humans are part of the organization's resource and where it does make a contribution and investment into each individual through the provision of benefits and training, talent possessed by people is an organizational resource.

Individual employees do, however, have freedom to choose what they do with their talents, at least in so far as opportunities provide people with the opportunity to develop it and use it. However, talent can also be wasted. This isn't about forcing people to do jobs that they have no desire to do; an individual might have a talent for creating spreadsheets, but it doesn't mean that they wish to have a career focused on developing spreadsheets, rather, a proposition that organizations have a responsibility to help individuals to release their talent potential and use their talent. The waste of talent is similar to the misuse of a natural asset, foolishly wasting nonreplaceable natural assets or the plundering of natural resources that should be saved for future generations, such a waste is surely intolerable.

Sustainability

Contemporary organizations have been dominated by managerialism and a focus on lean and efficient processing. It is not that lean processing does not have value to offer and organization, it does. However, the sustainability of cutting, delayering and reduction is rarely challenged. Not everything from a lean processing perspective makes sense from a human behavior perspective. For example, clear desks are certainly efficient but personalization helps individuals to feel as if they belong and are routed. Hot decking allows an organization to adopt flexible work practices, matrix working and fluid agile project teams, but not having a permanent place of work reduces loyalty and employee engagement. Like all these elements of the organizational system, these tensions need to be kept in balance. The implementation of lean processing within an organization is so often led by individuals who are fanatical and focused on beautiful processes and procedures but who fail to remember that processes are implemented by people, and if people are not bought into the process then no amount of painfully constructed best operating practices and policies showing flow charts is going to drive the correct behavior in the business. Lean process development cannot be dismissed simply as internal naval gazing, but organizations must also avoid forgetting that in the brave new digital economy, external influences on organizational activity can very quickly result in processes becoming obsolete. Minimal viable product (MVP) was introduced by Reis (2009), who suggested that a process of agile development was necessary. Sustainability does not mean remaining static, but ensuring that the way in which resources are allocated ensures the long-term survival of the organization. Organizations are adept at developing methods to track, monitor, and manage data to provide evidence of what needs to be done next. Big Data is introducing a realm of new information that managers can access to understand what their customers are thinking, accessing, and commenting on. Data analytics and data science are commonly used to demonstrate where organizations need to improve, but "when organizations are saturated with data, why don't insights emerge? Is it the wrong data? Is it a lack of time, capability and/or confidence to challenge upwards? For optimal impact, organizations need to constantly review and cull data collection processes that don't add value. An overemphasis on backward-looking targets defends existence but doesn't prove worth. Rather, organizations need to use the data, make the connections and be curious to uncover real insight" (CIPD, 2011). There needs to be acknowledgment that sustainability doesn't simply require the organization to sustain its internal processes and modes of operation, that agility and change is a significant part of organizational husbandry and as such must be seen as a tool and not an outcome that must be protected. Processes improvement, data analytics, organizational restructures, and more, result in additional layers of management science and complexity but fail to tap into the rich knowledge and experience that the people within the organization hold. Knowing when processes and policies are getting in the way of organizational development and impacting on the long-term survival of the organization is key outcome of organizational husbandry.

Organizational Husbandry and Purpose

If organizational husbandry is purposeful, then sustainability is achieved by accepting that it is necessary to go beyond today's strategy and process and ensure that agility is applied when using organizational resources. It is important that the organization uses its core sources to remain singularly focused on the achievement of the organization's reasons for being, not preserve today's policy, process, or way of doing things. Purposeful endeavor is more than a feeling that an organization should head in a particular direction. Instead, it is a permanent squid eye focused on truth of where the organization is now, compared to where the organization wishes to be. There can be no half measures, and sacred cows will need to be sacrificed in dedicating resources to the long-term direction of the organization, and at times that means losing in the short term.

Organizational Husbandry and the Leader in Me

Leaders of Expertise can help the organization to understand what resources are available and how to extract the most value from them. They must use their knowledge and understanding of best practice and emerging innovation, technology, and thinking to apply the "what next" to the organization setting. This involves being unrelenting in the pursuit of what fits the organizational best in terms of getting from where it is currently to where it wishes to be. Working alongside experts, leaders of people can contribute to the creation of an environment of sustainable performance but nurturing the human resource and ensuring that the environment helps each individual to achieve their full purpose.

Organizational Husbandry and the Talent Within

It is essential that the organization arouse curiosity among leaders about what talent resource is available to the organization and provoke individuals to seek out what their talent is. Unless there is a significant emphasis on the importance of knowing what talent resource is available and a determined effort to understand how the resource can be harnessed talent will remain an enigma. In essence, the organization must take steps to create an environment where individuals can achieve their full potential and, as a result, release the talent potential with the organization itself. This has the added benefit of improve self-actualization and releasing individuals to bring their full authentic self into the workplace. Increased employee engagement and improved levels of employee motivation are all positive side effects of such an endeavor.

Organizational Husbandry and Harmonious Communities

The richness of the organizational environment and the depth of relationships across the organization are essential if people are to really take note of what can be achieved together for the good of the organization, society, and individual. Developing a belief that together something greater can be achieved, that united is better than disparate, is more than the development of slogans. It is enabling people to work alongside each other, allowing time resource to be spent on dialogue and relationships development and creating spaces whether togetherness is achievable. Open-plan offices may put everyone together in the same space, but if the systems and processes drive individual result-seeking behaviors then resource will be wasted. Strong teams, and a strong identification with being part of something bigger than self, will help to drive positive organizational behaviors. Also, the organization must understand the value of wider community and responsibility to the society in which it operates. Organizational operations do not stop at the factory gates; employees are part of the wider community and ensuring the organization acts fairly, ethically, and responsibly is at the core of organizational husbandry.

Organizational Husbandry and Organizational Habitat

Human ergonomics is the study of how humans physically interact with the environment in a way which is responsive and develops productive behaviors. Creating an environment where people can thrive goes beyond simply making sure the desk height is comfortable or the chair prevents backache. There are strong links to ecology and enhancing the work environment to drive natural productive behaviors. This includes the use of light, temperature, utilizing different materials, and flow. Habitat also looks beyond the organization's office or factory and measures the impact of organizational operations on nature and natural resources. Depletion of natural resources may be unavoidable, but minimizing operations impact is more than being green, it is being creative and innovative in balancing profit with sustainability. Therefore, when it comes to environmental impacts, the focus needs to be not just inputs and outputs, but long-term outcomes that are sustainable.

Organizational Husbandry and Creative Adaptation

Releasing the full talent resource will encourage innovation and creativity, but being creative about how to deliver a profitable business while protecting resources needs dedicated resource to think, create, and experiment.

This requires the organization to ask the big questions, refusing to accept what is as "just the way it is," thus demanding people to demand more of themselves and others. Sometimes this creativity may be a short-term fix to a complex problem, other times it will be a complex solution to a long-term problem. How can we do this better will always lead to creative solutions, for example, energy efficiency and different materials.

Organizational Husbandry and Energy Transformation

Organization husbandry ensures that any energy expended adds values rather than reduces the value impact, that what resource is assigned to a venture, once expended, adds more to the business than it costs. Husbandry ensures that the organization is delivering what intends to, and the end result is a positive rather than a negative energy transformation. This means that activity adds to, and does not take away from the organization's overall value, this calculation may require longer-term interventions rather than quarterly short-term targets to allow investments to embed and deliver a return. Whatever the approach, the net result should be that the intervention drives the organization forward, even when facing difficult circumstances. Pay-off isn't always measured in profit or revenue, but the outcome does need to be positive and add something *more* than the organization was lacking previously.

Organizational Husbandry and Organizational Cycling

Organization husbandry is not a missive to preserve the status quo, but ensuring the survival of the organization for future generations. This includes the proactive adoption of changes, scanning the environment to remain ahead of the curve, and avoiding stagnation. Experimentation, creativity, and agility are key components of the mix, and adopting MVP practices will ensure the organization can respond to customer demands and actions by competitors to avoid becoming obsolete. Moving forward and ensuring the system is in motion will avoid complacency and a slow death rattle. Sustainability is ensuring the organizational outcomes remain fit for purpose and husbandry is delivering prosperity in the future as well as now.

Summary

- Organizational husbandry considers the moral duties that organizations have toward stakeholders and the wider society.
- Organizations operate in a social context and every organization has the responsibility for delivering sustainable processes and practices.
- Organizational husbandry is that it is people-centered and therefore its core value is that people are valuable and have value beyond something that can be measured purely financially.
- The organization has a social agenda in addition to an economic agenda.
- There have been numerous studies that demonstrate that sustainability is good for business.
- We must accept that we do not have true ownership of the natural resources, but rather, that we are loaned them for a period of time.

CHAPTER 8

Creative Adaptation

Response to External Changes

One of the attributes CEOs think is most important is creativity because if things are really complex, you can't pop out of business school with a predefined approach for dealing with a predefined problem. You've got to have creativity to be able to think

—Tony Bingham

The global market place coupled with the fast pace of technological change means that innovation and creativity are key attributes of both individuals and organizations wishing to navigate the choppy waters of modern economy. An organization must develop the capability to continually and swiftly move the way it operates, to shift toward the favorable wind like a ship changing its sail. This involves developing the creative capability to continually innovate organizational operations to shift toward favorable and sustainable performance as the result of changes taking place in the external environment and, more importantly, being able to proactively manage changes rather than react to changes thrust upon the organization. But words like agility, creativity, and innovation are easy to say, but developing the capacity to deliver these into a tangible force for creative adaptation takes more than a sexy slogan on a mission statement.

Creative adaptation is a strategic approach to organizational operations, which must be supported by the wider system, including people's capability to flex and adapt to changing demands, a structure that allows movement of ideas and people without burdensome organizational restructures, a supply chain that works in unison with the organization, and the freedom to experiment without fear of repercussions. This requires the organization to not only say that innovation and creative activity are important, but they must also develop a methodology and methods to allow organizational resources to be able to respond to external forces using creative adaptation.

The organization's vision provides the focus and inspiration for creative thinking and innovation throughout organizational operations as the managers and individual employees pursue opportunities to succeed in achieving the purpose of the organization. An essential source of competitive advantage, creativity, is highly prized in organizations where the development of useful knowledge and ideas is the result of the contributions of individuals. Creativity is a collaborative process, and involves corridor conversations and employees bouncing ideas of each other in the coffee bar. Creativity therefore requires the enabling of informal networks and flexibility to allow individuals to identify and solve problems and unearth new opportunities.

Organizational Operating Environment

Foster (2017d) wrote about the organizational operating environment. The greatest change in the organizational environment is what technology has done to the way people think about and interact with organizations. It's no longer about bargaining power or threat or positive forces or negative forces, rather the new reality is about connection, interconnection, interdependence, and dependence (see Figure 8.1).

Connection

Seeking purposeful existence isn't limited to those with a religious faith. It is at the center of what makes us human. Maslow's Hierarchy of Needs (1943) may be a bit tired when discussing employee motivation, but he did identify the need for purposeful endeavor. Organizations are constructed by the way people who are connected with it discuss why it exists and what it is seeking to achieve. If people share the organizational purpose, then they are connected to the organization beyond a simple transactional relationship; it is meaningful. This connection is not limited to

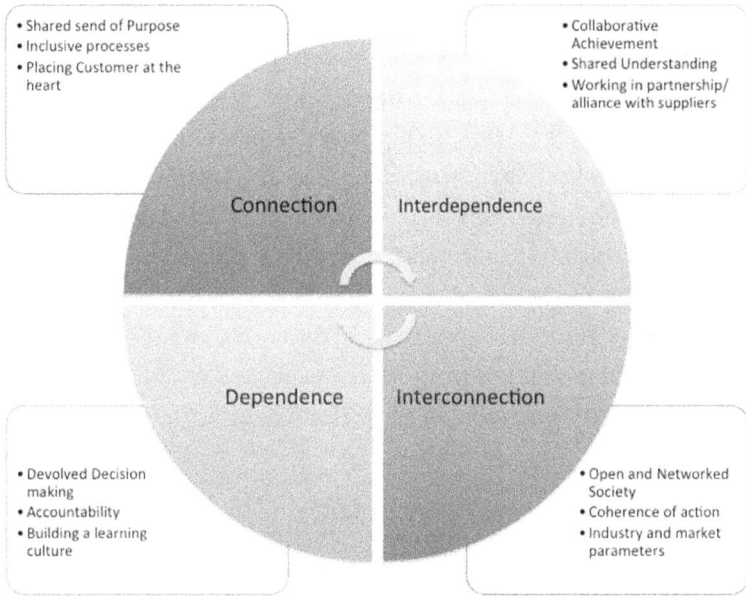

- Shared send of Purpose
- Inclusive processes
- Placing Customer at the heart

- Collaborative Achievement
- Shared Understanding
- Working in partnership/ alliance with suppliers

Connection   Interdependence

Dependence   Interconnection

- Devolved Decision making
- Accountability
- Building a learning culture

- Open and Networked Society
- Coherence of action
- Industry and market parameters

Figure 8.1 The organizational operating reality

employees working for an organization. Customers are seeking out organizations with which they can give meaning to their exchange. Customer relationships are no longer simply about keeping customers sweet so they buy your product or use your service again. They want to connect with what the organization is trying to achieve. On the some level, marketing has developed a process of creating meaning for products or services. They give us worth, or connect with us in terms of how we identify with who we are as individuals. Suppliers are looking to connect with organizations beyond a simplistic exchange of goods. They want to understand how they can be integrated into the supply chain, so there is little boundary between the supplier and the buyer. Connection therefore becomes about inclusivity, shared goals, and an existential understanding.

Interdependence

The economy is polarizing. On the one hand, there is monopolization as mergers and acquisitions lead to supra-global corporations, which are swallowing up the competition. Consumers might think they are choosing between competitors when, in fact, they are choosing from different brands owned by the same organization. However, at the same time, disruption to traditional markets and the way of doing business is taking place. This goes beyond new entrants, where in many cases the barriers to entry have disappeared completely and has transitioned to previously unthinkable strategic alliances, competitors working together, and partnership between suppliers and customers. The traditional boundaries of competitor and organization, supplier and customer, employee and employer have blurred and have changed the normal rules of engagement. The requirement is for leaders to create an environment where collaboration and a shared understanding of what can be achieved is the norm.

Dependence

The speed of change within organizations today means that the hierarchical structure of decision making is with the leader at the top and the employees at the bottom waiting for diktats to cascade is no longer sustainable. Change isn't so much planned but rather a coordinated series of leaps of invention, reinvention, innovation, and inspired imagination. There is a need for leaders to have a confidence in decision making at all levels within the organization, relying on those closest to the problems to have the wherewithal to manage and respond to opportunities and challenges as they arise. The leader's role, therefore, is to create an organizational framework that encourages an environment where employees are free to experiment, share, gain, discard, and evolve their knowledge, skills, and experience to be battle ready at all times. In the same way, teams should no longer be considered as fixed entities. Instead, groups will come together and dissolve as agents of enterprise as they respond to the demands from the environment.

Interconnection

It was only in 1991 that the World Wide Web became publicly available, transforming the way business operates, employee's work and how customers, suppliers, and competitors interact, and in fact it changed society forever. The digital age has transmuted networks from fairly simple channels of linear back-and-forth communication. A complex web of relationships, composed of interconnections between personal, social, and professional parts is held on digital devices that fit into someone's back pocket, the Connectors' (Gladwell, 2002) little black book has been replaced by friends, followers, and links. Organization's themselves have access and open networks with individual customers, potential suppliers, and competitors in ways that have never before been possible. This presents a unique opportunity and a huge challenge. Controlling the message requires a coherence of action, which no longer has the benefit of communication gatekeepers. Every single employee becomes the voice of the organization and every interaction a chance for corporate purgatory or Elysium. In addition, surety about industry sectors and market parameters has blurred at the edges, extending into a labyrinth of systems of interconnection.

Innovation Is a Way of Life

The Organizational Operating Reality (OOR) demands creative adaptation, agility, innovation, and creativity to become essential components of an organizational framework that can respond to the challenges and opportunities presented, create competitive advantage in a complex climate, and develop a system where the organizational resources are employed effectively. Lawler III (2008) stated that, "creative destruction means that organizations that don't adapt to changes in their environment ultimately lose out because new organizations that better fit the current environment outperform them. New organizations often have a significant competitive advantage simply because they are created, conceptualized and designed with the current environment in mind" (Lawler III, 2008). The OOR has changed and is changing rapidly. It is not a case of developing a readiness of change, but willingly and deliberately building the energy and capability for creative adaptation. It goes beyond simply managing communication and delivers a purposefully constructed uninterrupted channel of communication to extended networks, both within the organization and externally.

Most organizations wish to be associated with innovation, whether it is by being first to market with a new product or service, finding competitive advantage through innovative responses to customer needs, developing innovative marketing techniques, or delivering innovative methods to run the business. The idea is to inspire loyalty among their customer base, employees, suppliers, and shareholders by being ahead of the curve. To be innovative, an organization must first of all make the decision that is it is going to be innovate; that is, giving individuals within the organization freedom to spend time and resources getting creative, trying out new ways of doing things, and giving people access to combine know-how with others. Without creative activity, making time to question the norm, contemplate the future, and look "out there" organizations will not build the capability internally for innovation.

Innovation is often seen as that spark of inspiration that comes to someone in a moment and drives the organization forward. Beswick (2011) described innovation as "the successful exploitation of an idea that adds value to the customer and commercial return for the creator. Anything that can be described as an innovation needs to add value. It could change the way business works so that it becomes more efficient (and therefore more profitable), it could change the way people are managed and motivated (and therefore retain and attract staff, reducing recruitment costs) or it could be a new product or service that helps drive customer spend and generate sustainable and profitable returns" (Beswick, 2011). But ideas don't come out of nowhere and are the product of having the opportunity to explore, experiment, and create free from the fetters of how things are currently done. Space to think is especially rare in Western organizations. Often comparisons are drawn between office spaces in Western corporations versus that in their Eastern counterparts. If the boss walks by, Westerners work hard to look busy, woe betides anyone who is just sat at their desk daydreaming. No, in Western offices, desks are often cluttered with various projects that the busy bees are working on. In Eastern business cultures, desks are generally clear of clutter and room is given for just sitting and contemplating. Just imagine an office where you are encouraged to sit quietly and meditate on a problem. Even Western ideation is based on the idea of brainstorming and active rambunctious process with people shouting out to be heard. It is hardly a quiet concept encouraging people to be in quiet or deep contemplation.

Innovation and creativity require space and time for people to cogitate. It is a little like the compost heap, lots of rubbish gets thrown on top, which requires time to break down, and it is only after a period of time, composting, that the mineral and nutrient-rich soil that is needed for growth is developed. But how does this marry with the need to be agile and responsive in a fast-moving environment.

The secret is, according to Beswick (2011), "to buy into my philosophy that 'innovation is a by-product of being exceptional' and that unless we strive to be outrageously good at what we do the chances of us being truly different, innovative and world class are remote" (Beswick, 2011). This means, of course, that innovation is a way of life. It isn't something the organization only does in response to an immediate threat or problem. People, throughout the organization, would have already spent time thinking about the various problems that might occur, so when the problem does occur, there is already an answer ready to go, or, at the very least, a number of options that can be worked on to develop further.

Constant scanning, access to the latest thinking; ongoing dialogue and debate; and freedom to explore, experiment, and learn shouldn't be the preserve of itinerant workers, or those in the upper echelons of the organization. It should be the Alpha and the Omega of the way in which the organization operates. An employee population following a leader who is never satisfied with the status quo and always working on the next big thing.

Creativity and Collaboration

An essential source of competitive advantage, creativity is highly prized in organizations where the development of useful knowledge and ideas is the result of the contributions of individuals throughout the organization. Creativity is a collaborative process and involves corridor conversation and bouncing ideas of each other in the coffee bar or round the water cooler. Creativity therefore requires the enabling of informal networks and flexibility to allow individuals to identify and solve problems and unearth new opportunities. These networks have to be constructed deliberately and be part of a strategic plan to extend the knowledge of individuals, teams, and the organization as a whole beyond its current parameters. Networks of collaboration are built by enabling those who are naturally good at connecting with others, the freedom to establish wider networks and encouraging those who are not, to access networks that are already established by others will widen access to new knowledge and thinking to bring into the organizational habitat. In addition to relying on individuals, organizational leaders and teams will need to be deliberate on aligning the organization with various think tanks, trade bodies, and industry networks to ensure that the organization is up to date on what is occurring outside of its boundaries. Ensuring that employees are able to volunteer to sit on trade boards, advisory committees, and industry panels as part of their personal and career development plans will also ensure that the organization is well represented when new industry challenges are being discussed.

Working in partnership or in an alliance with other organizations will also enable the organization to access expertise from other interested parties and enable creativity from cross-fertilization of ideas. Innovation is not always invention, but the combination of two existing things to make a new thing. This brings a new dimension to partnerships and alliance when working together to solve a common problem.

Regardless of who is involved in the collaboration, the key to creative adaptation is being allowed to ask awkward questions and for curiosity to be encouraged. If the questions are painful or challenging, they are probably the most important questions that need to be asked, and leaders of the organization shouldn't shush people or try and avoid answering the question, especially if the truthful answer to the question is "I don't know." Freedom must be given to find answers to the questions that no one has answers to, and that sometimes means dedicated organizational budget for research and development to pursue the answers to challenging questions.

Adaptation Not Evolution

When choosing the term creative adaptation to describe this element of organizational balance, I was aware that adaptation may indicate an evolutionary process. The word adaptation refers to a process of alteration in the structure or operation of an organization as whole or in part, which enables the organization to be better fitted to survive in the competitive environment. This isn't the same as evolution, which refers to change over a long period of time. Lawler III (2008) warns against organizational evolution stating that, "slow change is a sure route to business failure. Being able to change quickly and effectively has become a basic requirement or organization capability in today's business environment" (Lawler III, 2008). Building creative adaptation into the everyday tasks allows the organization to be both forward looking and responsive. Regardless of the challenges the organization faces, if the attitude and behaviors within the organization are that of adaptation, that is, making the necessary alterations to survive, then that is an ongoing process of learning. Argyris and Schon (1996) introduced the concept of double-loop learning, which is related to the practice of critical reflection, because it explicitly explores and evaluates a situation based on existing conceptualizations, underlying organizational assumptions, and consideration of the consequences of the actions taken. This will include a confrontation of existing assumptions, values, beliefs, and biases as a result of social, economic, and political context that is considered necessary for improved organizational performance. Creative adaptation is a continuous process of double-loop learning whereby the employees and leaders within the organization work in a critically reflective way that results in unlearning existing paradigms and learning what is necessary to adapt to new conditions.

How to Create Creative Adaptation Capability

The key to creative adaptation is to give people something that organizations have so often resisted: time and resource. It doesn't have to be significant, but time and resource does need to be invested in enabling employees to extend their technical knowledge in their field of expertise, discipline, or area of specialization, connect with others, perhaps in communities of practice and get access to what is going on in the rest of the world. This also involves the creation of knowledge-gathering and knowledge-sharing processes to monitor new advances in the industry and changes in the competitive environment. This goes beyond a simple PEST analysis for an annual strategic review. It is a way of doing business that gathers and shares information continuously and, more importantly, feeds that into day-to-day operations. Individuals are given time capacity to take this information and think about it. Whether in groups, using tools such as Action Learning Set (ALS) or Appreciative Inquiry (AI) or providing individuals with scheduled time to *be* creative, creative adaptation needs to be intentional, institutionalized, and pursued.

ALS, which involves small groups of learners who gather to share experience in the workplace, encourages set members to act on their learning. Active membership of an ALS aids creative adaptation by enabling individuals to learn from what they do in their current practice, what they have learned from the external environment, and examine ways in which improvements can be made. An ALS is made up of between 6 and 12 members, who meet for a minimum of 3 hours, usually with an independent facilitator to support set members as they work on a presented problem through supportive, but probing, questioning. Members support the person with the presenting problem to find their own solution, encouraging members to reflect upon real-time issues within the workplace and analyzing possible solutions.

AI facilitates groups in order that they may generate new ideas through a form of inquiry that focuses on the positive or the appreciative. The purpose of the AI process is to enable the group to recognize the best of people and the organization. This systematic exploration results in organizational learning and creativity. The process utilizes the positive potential of human imagination and innovation aimed at the whole organization, teams, function, or department using dialogue to help focus on what is right and creating an imagined future.

Workplace Play

If you think about your life, and when you were at your most free creativity, it was likely when you were still a child. Whether it is the education system or life, in general, as we grow up we lose the freedom we had to create unabashed by what people think, or how we are judged. Even those with creative talent are urged to get a "proper" job and stop "playing around" as they leave school and enter adulthood. Within an organization, there is no doubt a contingent of people who should be artists, actors, carpenters, and writers who are administrators or managers because they need to earn a living. Encouraging them to be true to who they are sits within the chapter on Talent Within, but the importance of play belongs here in creative adaptation. As young children, we are encouraged to pretend play, use our imagination, and explore the impossible. But as we get older, we get criticized for acting like children if we have too much fun or play the child. This shuts down a unique bond between play, imagination, and creativity. Russ and Wallace (2013) state that, "theorists and researchers in the fields of child development, child psychotherapy, creativity, personality, and evolution have reached the conclusion that pretend play and creativity are linked." How freely we are able to be creative is a result of how free we were to play in our childhood. But this isn't a one-shot deal. Once you are grown up, you have missed your chance to learn how to be creative. Play allows us to develop "divergent thinking, broad associative skill, insight, cognitive flexibility, and perspective taking" (Russ and Wallace, 2013), the very essence of creative adaptation. It may have come to your attention that companies with a legacy in creativity and younger employees have play built into the architecture of their business. Whether slides in the office, games rooms, or adult playgrounds outside. Play doesn't have to be so . . . obvious. However, acknowledging that play is important in driving creative adaptation and providing room for play to be part of the lexicon of the business is an essential component. This might be to use Lego, craft materials, or games during facilitated sessions to get people to jump out of linear thinking patterns, or introducing creative opportunities for all employees in their day-to-day interactions, for example, the introduction of graffiti walls. Offering space and time for play will aid the attitudes, behaviors, and thinking needed for creative adaptation to become a real way of doing business.

Creative Adaptation and Purpose

Creating an environment whereby creative adaptation is acknowledged and encouraged. It is not just about ensuring that employees have the skills or knowledge to be creative or that the organization's leadership has the motivation and ability to communicate and drive the adaptation required. It is the link to the purpose of the organization is made and the understanding of the need to practice creative adaptation is at a meaningful level, encouraging individuals to choose to engage with the process of innovation and creativity.

Creative Adaptation and the Leader in Me

Leaders have a dual responsibility. First, they must practice creativity in their own work life, being role models to the rest of the employee population. Perhaps being seen in meditative contemplation or pondering life's bigger questions with individuals. The second responsibility is, by leading by example, also using their power and authority to make it okay to think, create, and play in the workplace. This includes releasing budget and increasing head count to make space for creativity.

Creative Adaptation and the Talent Within

Some people will find creative adaptation a welcome boon to their day-to-day job role. For others it will be like walking through the very gates of hell. Recognizing that for some people creativity is needed and fulfills their authentic self means giving them extra space to go the extra mile on behalf of the organization. However, for those who feel awkward or uncomfortable, there must equally be a recognition that this doesn't sit within their frame. Understanding that the creativity comes in different guises is important in establishing creative adaptation in line with individual comfort levels. Recognizing that creativity isn't linked to craft skills or being an artist is also essential.

Creative Adaptation and Harmonious Communities

Creating space and time for individuals to come together in informal groups and formal team setting that allow them to bounce ideas of each other, introduce new discovers, and explore problems in a safe environment is essential. Giving people room to work with who they choose, who they connect with, regardless of reporting lines and organizational structure is essential to support cross-fertilization of knowledge and develop adaptive processes and technology.

Creative Adaptation and Organizational Habitat

Environment is essential to creativity. It is difficult to create in a dark dingy office space with gray walls and poor lighting. If that is the only office space you have, then developing opportunities to go off site and be inspired elsewhere is essential. Taking trips to other spaces, whether public buildings or other organizations for case study visits, is a cheap and useful tactic to get people out of an environment that may be suppressing their creative thinking. Developing quiet outside spaces are beneficial, or at the very least, highlighting areas of natural beauty that employees can walk or cycle will give people places to go. Developing a lunch break policy that forces people away from their desk will also help to force individuals out of rigid routines and thinking.

Creative Adaptation and Organizational Husbandry

Creative adaptation is the workhorse behind organizational husbandry. Adapting to the demands from external environmental pressures through proactive, continuous creativity, innovation, and agility will enable the organization to be sustained in the long term. But the practice of creative adaptation also needs to be sustained, and as such cannot become a "flavor of the month" business practice, it needs to become a way of doing business practice.

Creative Adaptation and Energy Transformation

Tapping into the creative within the workforce means that different techniques will need to be used to find the one that delivers the most return on investment. Different networking events or activities will lead to different outcomes. Ensuring that in the review of any activity there is an evaluation of the value added to the organization will ensure that time and resource invested isn't wasted. Keeping track of the outcomes of creative adaptation will help ensure that future investment is supported throughout the organization and by the variety of stakeholders concerned with the organization's success.

Creative Adaptation and Organizational Cycling

Creative adaptation is the tool that can be used to respond to the forces that are impacting on the organizational balance. There is also a need for recognition that any input from creative adaptation also has an output that affects organizational balance. The ideal situation would be that just as pressures from outside the organization enforce an imbalance, creative adaptation rebalances through the introduction of innovation, the use of creativity, or the agility with which the organization can respond to the pressure. What is essential is that creative adaptation does not take place in a vacuum or through a process of internal navel gazing. Instead, employees throughout the organization are encouraged and empowered through being fully briefed about what is happening out there in order to develop creative responses to possible pressures.

Summary

- An organization must develop the capability to continually and swiftly move the way it operates.
- Organizations must develop a methodology and methods to allow organizational resources to be able to respond to external forces using creative adaptation.
- Creativity requires the enabling of informal networks and flexibility to allow individuals to identify and solve problems and unearth new opportunities.
- Freedom must be given to find answers to the questions that no one has answers to.
- The greatest change in the organizational environment is what technology has done to the way people think about and interact with organizations. The new reality is about connection, interconnection, interdependence, and dependence.
- The word adaptation refers to a process of alteration in the structure or operation of an organization as whole or in part, which enables the organization to be better fitted to survive in the competitive environment.

- Creative adaptation is a continuous process of double-loop learning.
- The key to creative adaptation is time and resource.

Play is important in driving creative adaptation and providing room for play to be part of the lexicon of the business is an essential component.

CHAPTER 9

Energy Transformation

The Value Chain

Productivity is never an accident. It is always the result of a commitment to excellence, intelligent planning, and focused effort.

—Paul J. Meyer

When exploring the idea of organization balance it should be noted that given the natural order of things, any activity that the organization engages in will lead to disorder. As such the organization must be committed to evaluating whether the actions that have been taken are having the impact they should be having, assessing that the time and resource (energy) committed is delivering added value and that the energy expended is positively and sustainably transforming the performance within the organization.

The question that an organization needs to ask itself is whether what it is doing as an organization is having the desired impact and, more importantly, whether the activity is aligned to the core purpose. This is about the need to understand at all levels of the organization whether individual and group actions and activities are having the impact it should be having, that the time and resource (energy) committed are delivering the desired outcome, and the result is transforming the organization to be in balance rather than in crisis, sustainable rather than short-term improvements with long-term issues. Furthermore, it is about ensuring that the sum of the organization's parts is more than the whole.

Activity Leads to Disorder

Eventually, whatever it is that human activity produces results in an outcome or output that is dispersed into its surroundings whether that is physical or in the form of mental or emotional energy. It might seem talking about an organization producing energy that isn't just a physical form. However, organizations can be a force for good, or for evil. They can positively affect the individual employees who work for the organization or negatively affect their lives. Consider, if you will when an individual is offered a job at an organization. If it is a job they wish to do, that fulfills their full self, that is, a positive intervention in their life and the life of their friends and family. The salary they earn contributes to the wider society, ensuring the employment of others as they buy products and services, leading to a virtuous circle of positivity. However, think about what happens if an organization offers a job to an individual, who hands in their notice at their current employment. Imagine if the day before the individual is due to start their new job, the organization withdraws the offer. This isn't the stuff of fiction. This is a real-life situation that was shared recently on LinkedIn. The impact that the organization has had on that individual isn't just physical, in that, that person who thought they were going to start a new job is now without a job. There is the added stress of loss of income, perhaps the impact on their spouse and children of such a situation. In the UK, if you resign from a position you can't claim job seekers' allowance for 2 months. Think also of the longer-term impact on that person's confidence, their emotional well-being as they navigate a situation that should never have happened.

This is a simple illustration, but the newspapers are full of stories of organizations that have destroyed lives, the courts full of litigation because of poor management, environmental damage, and health-endangering activities, many of which could have been avoided if only care had been taken not just of the economics but of the emotional and mental well-being of people.

Therefore, any activity that the organization does leads to some kind of disorder. It may not be intentional or malicious, but it impacts much more widely and is more consequential than perhaps we might imagine—whether it is the impact of gathering raw materials, logistics, production, or supply, through to the impact on people within the supply chain. But disorder does not need to be a negative thing. It is a disruption to the way in which things were once ordered or the systematic functioning that is disrupted. If the broadband is systematically functioning at 1.5mb and a supplier change improves internet speed to 50mb, the systematic functioning of the broadband has been disrupted, but the person using the internet will be delighted at how fast their internet is working. Disruption is not a bad thing. However, recognizing that each interaction leads to disruption perhaps makes people more aware of the kind of disruption being created.

Reviewing the disruption that has occurred, for good or bad, is a central component of organizational balance. By engaging in action and activity, whether at an individual level, team level, or organizational level, we must be cognizant that change will occur. The responsibility of the organization, its leaders and employees, is to ensure that as much as possible that change is positive.

Diffusion of Interventions

Diffusion of interventions happens when changes made in one area of organizational activity is transferred from one part of the system to another. It is not possible to target human activity precisely to cure a problem. For example, medicine might be able to produce treatments that can target cancers; however, the cancer, when destroyed, is dispersed within the body. Like many things, most activity can be dispersed in a way that does not affect the organization as a whole; like dropping 10ml of orange juice into a bath of water wouldn't warrant much notice. But the amount of activity that takes place in an organization means that the likely contamination of the balance of the organization is increased. Understanding that what begins as a seemingly benign activity with little consequence can, through the process of energy transformation, build into a sizable contaminant. It may build over a long period of time, barely noticeable for those in the middle of the change taking place, when suddenly what was seemingly inconsequential becomes devastating. It is therefore incumbent upon the organization that every interaction, every action, and every activity is focused on delivering a positive result, and minute it changes, the early warning signs are not ignored if the activity is having a negative affect.

Diffusion isn't just about organizational activity. Individual interactions with people also have a consequence. Everyone can make mistakes, but if issues become patterns of behavior then ignoring them or hoping they would go away won't reduce the impact of the problem. We must challenge ourselves to be aware of our own impact on others. How our actions are diffused and thus develop energy signatures of their own.

Promoting Positivity

Although positivity has been heavily criticized as ignoring problems, in the context of organizational balance, positivity is about individuals being empowered to approach opportunities and challenges with confidence and optimism, Energy transformation remains positive as long as activity enables the organization to develop a culture of possibility both within individuals and within teams. On an individual level, corporate life is made up of two types of people: energy givers and energy vampires. Energy givers are those people who walk into a room and infuse the room with their positivity and energy. Their personal impact is immediate and long lasting; people come away from interactions with energy givers and feel motivated, mobilized, and believe that a problem can be overcome and opportunity can be won, and all things are possible. The insurmountable problem that is being faced suddenly appears like a molehill, easily dealt with, and coupled with the energy and plan to create an opportunity that is completely achievable. Energy givers create sparks of innovation and creativity; they provide a get up a go to other people, meaning that forward momentum and activity happens around them.

Energy vampires literally suck the life out of the room and anyone who is foolish enough to engage with them. They sit in corners of the office, usually with a large winter coat zipped right up to their nose, probably a big wooly scarf and ensuring everyone within earshot is aware of their issue with the temperature of the air conditioning. They feed off of and destroy the joy and energy of others. Vampires cast a dark shadow, which accompanies their workspace, and if the team is unlucky enough, it begins to spread like a fungus across the office, killing the energy, optimism, and the lifeblood of an organization. Both energy vampires and energy givers disrupt the organization setting; vampires use energy to destroy projects, whereas givers impact the atmosphere of the organization in such a way that their interactions enrich people.

Positivity is a choice; it's not about the way we are born or the mood we are in. We can choose to be more positive, and in the same way, organizations can choose to have a positive effect through the choice of interventions and monitoring the disruption that its energy releases.

Energy Transformation

Energy transformation is strongly linked to the purpose of the organization and what it is that the organization is trying to achieve. If the purpose is negative, then the outcome will be negative. However, energy transformation is a determination that, regardless of the input the transformation process leading to outcomes, will disrupt the world in a positive way. This will be through sustainable practices as discussed in organizational husbandry as well as in individual, group, and organizational interventions which in and of themselves are deliberately positive. This means for every action there needs to be an awareness of the reaction to that action. There is thoughtfulness in energy transformation that demands a responsibility and accountability for outcomes.

If the short-term outcome is unintentionally negative, then it is the organization that must invest to ensure that the medium- to long-term position is positive and that a thorough understanding of the systematic issues that led to the negative outcomes are processed and corrected. A process of continuous benchmarking and evaluation is therefore required to manage the performance of organizational activity. Russ-Eft (2014, 550) defines evaluation as "the systematic and on-going processes for gathering data about programs, organizations, and whole societies to enhance knowledge and decision making." In evaluating activity, there must be a review of the alignment of activity and practices to organizational values and purpose. The decision to evaluate how energy is transformed within the organization must be based on a systematic assessment methodology, focused on what the organization values, and the impact or outcome of the energy, which results in competitive advantage for the organization. Evaluation is also focused on what the organization, team, or individual has learned from their activity. In regard to organizational balance, evaluation is not the end process but a continuous process of measuring and intuiting what is happening within the organization. Like pollsters who are constantly taking the temperature of the country in regard to government, the organization must remain interested and determined to constantly seek to understand what is happening in the organization. In expending energy, has the organization achieved what they set out to achieve and what else has been achieved along the way? A runner may win a race, but along the way they may have learned about what nutrition works best, a better running technique, or an improvement in training methodology. It will be the smallest of the changes and shifts in an organization's balance, which will give clues as to what it really going on. Lagging performance figures such as financial data are purely an output of what has already gone before. For an organization to create the environment for adaptation, it must seek early indicators of system change.

To reiterate, the disruption can be positive, and in being so, actions and activities can be repeated if there is knowledge gathered regarding the disruptive action. This is the difference between causation and correlation. Correlation can be spurious, X and Y are correlated is separate from X causes Y. Delving in to the learning from how outcomes were achieved will provide information about how to repeat (or avoid) the outcome that has occurred, how to do it better next time, or highlight areas for improvement.

Energy Transformation and Purpose

Energy transformation demands that the organization ensures that the purposeful endeavor that it chooses is positively framed and positive in regard to the outcome it aims for. Knowing that any purposeful endeavor will lead to disruption, the organization should seek to have a positive disruptive influence, creating good ahead of bad.

Energy Transformation and the Leader in Me

Leaders at the very least must not be energy vampires and must develop themselves to be self-aware of the impact that they have on others. Leaders should choose to be energy givers in every interaction with their line reports, peers, and key stakeholders. Not just when it is going well, but when things aren't going well and even more so when things are going very badly. The leader is the one who needs to stand there in the middle of the worse crisis and say, okay this is bad, but we can get through this; there is a solution, a way out, and a possibility for redemption. Even when everyone else around them is losing their head, and when the leaders themselves have no clue what the next step is, they must choose a positive attitude and expect it of others.

Energy Transformation and the Talent Within

As with leaders, the same is true for the Talent Within. Choosing optimism rather than pessimism, choosing hope rather than hopelessness, choosing positivity rather than negativity is within the power of every individual to choose to develop positivity as an attitude. Since attitude is a choice; the choice to be an energy giver is possible. This isn't about personality or character. Some individuals might be generally inclined to being an energy giver, for others the choice must be conscious; however, it is still a choice that anyone can make.

Energy Transformation and Harmonious Communities

Teams and groups must work together, pooling their resources, knowledge, and skills to overcome problems and plan for what is coming down the line. This means they must be aware of what is happening elsewhere, the impact of their actions and activities on other departments, teams, and the wider society. Departments and functions are not in competition with each other where there are winners and losers, instead they must work to ensure that every action results in a win–win for all sides.

Energy Transformation and Organizational Habitat

The organization's environment and its structure will impact on the effect that an action or intervention will have on other parts of the organization and the external environment, for example, if customer service is working to be agile and innovative, developing a positive response to customer queries and complaints. But the process of taking the query or complaint and doing something with it prevents what has agreed from happening, then the positivity of the interaction with the customer service team can become negative due to the inaction of the production team. All elements of the organization must be aware of the diffusion of their actions on the system and process as a whole. Sometimes this means that certain processes has no benefit for the person at the input end, it's just another task that needs to be completed, but the result of getting the input right will positively affect the diffusion of the intervention in delivering a favorable output.

Energy Transformation and Organizational Husbandry

Negative diffusion of intervention is not sustainable. Therefore, a balance must be struck between short-and long-term outcomes, and pressure to deliver a result or target must be resisted if through its delivery long-term results will be poorly affected. This is very often seen in efficient versus effectiveness scenarios where cheaper in the short-term results in poor value in the longer term. Balancing budgetary constraints with the right thing to do for the long term will be an on-going issue in fighting to achieve organizational balance.

Energy Transformation and Creative Adaptation

Negativity is not conducive to an innovative or a creative mindset, promoting the positive will have a powerful effect on creative adaptation. At the same time, dealing with experimentation and exploration that leads nowhere or goes wrong means a growth or learning mindset is as important as getting it right each time. When it comes to research and development, there is a requirement to manage risks and see failure as a positive step toward success.

Energy Transformation and Organizational Cycling

The organization is in a constant cycle of interaction with the external environment. Just as the organizational activities and actions cause disruption for others, external influences and the actions of other agencies or organizations can have a devastating impact upon the organization itself. Some of these disruptions are quite obvious, for example a hurricane or flooding destroying an organization's production plant. Others can be subtle or accumulate over time. For example, the UK government's decision to focus on examination results rather than deeper learning has resulted in a problem with younger people entering the workforce lacking the necessary employability skills. Understanding the external disruptions will help the organization to creatively adapt and continuously change in response.

Summary

- Given the natural order of things, any activity that the organization engages in will lead to disorder.
- Is what the organization is doing having a desired impact and more importantly whether activity is aligned to the core purpose?
- Reviewing the disruption that has occurred, for good or bad, is a central component of organizational balance.
- Diffusion of interventions happens when changes made in one area of organizational activity is transferred from one part of the system to another.
- Energy transformation remains positive as long as activity enables the organization to develop a culture of possibility both within individuals and within teams.
- Energy givers are those people who walk into a room and infuse the room with their positivity and energy.
- A process of continuous benchmarking and evaluation is therefore required to manage the performance of organizational activity.
- Correlation can be spurious.

CHAPTER 10

Organizational Cycling

The Influences on Organization Balance

Every living being is an engine geared to the wheelwork of the universe. Though seemingly affected only by its immediate surrounding, the sphere of external influence extends to infinite distance.

—Nikola Tesla

The requirement for sustainability is a mix of seemingly competing demands requiring resolution to create balance. There are many influences on organizational balance, forces that can cause disruption, lessons that can be learned, and the inversion of organizational development and design processes. In developing an organization design model based on balance, the question is whether it is achievable in a globalized marketplace. Whether it is the UK's decision to leave the European Union, the failure of the international community to tackle the crisis in Syria, or President Trump's bombastic approach to Iran and North Korea, the world is seemingly more volatile and chaotic than at any time since the Second World War.

Whether it is political, economic, social, or technical, every single day an organization will have an issue in one area or other, whether internal or external. The importance of balance can be found in the changes organizations are making in response to international trade cooperation, free movement of goods, service, capital, and people across country borders. The capitalist market system requires new markets across the global in order to deliver economic performance at local, regional, and national levels, and for each level there are winners and losers as a result. The implications for organizations are the dynamism of the business environment means balance must be fought for between in seemingly endless streams of competing demands requiring rebalancing.

Forces That Can Cause Disruption

The forces that can cause disruption therefore are varied. Since 2008 and the global financial credit crunch, there has been significant pressure building across the globe. In 2016 significant political shifts began to exert themselves in the West, including the decision by the UK to leave the European Union, the election of President Donald Trump, and the rejection of constitutional reforms in Italy. The shift from consensus and the increased risk of deglobalization was apparently halted with the election of French president Maron in 2017, but the rise of the alt-right in the United States, the far-right successes in the elections in Germany, and the declaration of independence in Catalonia appear to suggest that the disruption of populism is far from over. Geopolitical factors such as economic disparity between the have's and have not's, perceptions of governance failures by the ruling elite, the breakdown of community due to changing social value and persistent inequality based on race, gender, and sexuality is causing significant imbalance in the external macro economic environment.

What is certain is that change is inevitable. But change management does not have a good success rate. Hoey (2011) highlighted some key research statistics regarding change success outcomes:

- "75 per cent of change initiatives failed to reach their goals—Mourier and Smith *Conquering Organizational Change*
- 70 per cent of business change projects fail—John Kotter *Leading Change* Harvard Business School
- Only 30 percent of transformation projects succeed—McKinsey survey 2008
- 80 per cent of sales training does not achieve its goals—Dave Stein, ESR Research."

However, change management traditionally focuses on the techno-structural factors of an organization's design. Considering the factors that drive the need for change and regardless of the enormity of the disruptive forces that are taking place, acknowledgment must be made that they all have one thing in common. They have at their center human beings. Whether it is disruption caused by catastrophic weather events, the introduction of new technology or the aftereffects of violence, the focus of the event is about the human impact.

Designing for Performance

Performance management system design in organizations is excruciating. A frustrating tick box exercise where both line managers and employees go through the annual pain of filling in the required paperwork, because the organization has a performance management process or system rather than a performance management culture. Organizations spend millions on the latest super snazzy performance management software, but until they tackle the behavior and attitude around performance management they will continue to have ineffective management of performance in their business.

Designing organizational systems for performance requires a system in which the organization sets clear leadership expectations and outcomes, can flex to the needs of the individual, and develop each individual's unique talent set in line with the current and future capability requirements of the organization. A balanced system will enable the organization to organize capability and its people talent resource requirements. Leaders are the key to performance, but it is not about a performance appraisal system. Leaders need to role model the desired behaviors themselves, ensuring that they manage their own performance as part of their day-to-day activity and engaging and communicating with their own line manager. Leaders are custodians of performance design in the organization, since it is an essential skills requirement, if they are not setting and agreeing goals, empowering people, or celebrating success, they are not managing the performance of the people they are leading. The use of job descriptions built around the individual brings into special significance the importance of setting and agreeing objectives with the individual. Too often managers will set performance objectives that are the same for everyone in their team. In embracing the recognition of individual talent in the creation of job roles and allocation of tasks, the leader must ensure that objectives set and agreed are individual and hold relevance to the job the individual is required to perform in pursuit of the organizational purpose. The focus of organization design for performance is on the human.

Organization Development

The process that organizational development proposes is one that is oriented to organizational intervention in terms of the total organizational system as whole and its pursuit of organizational effectiveness using behavioral science practice that focused on human potential, participation, and development in order to bring changes to strategies, structures, and processes. Organizational Development practice provides tools that can be utilized to evaluate forces, that need rebalancing with the organizational context, and that release the potential within the organization for sustainable performance.

The cycling refers to the need for the adoption and adaptation in the balanced organization for continuous change. However, the OD processes of diagnosing, analyzing, designing, managing, and evaluating OD interventions splits the processes that affect the human factors from the technostructural processes. OD processes therefore support the organization in considering the human inputs that impact the organizational system. The CIPD stated that, "employees can be the early warning system—in other words, they can be the early detectors of threats and opportunities. Effective mechanisms for upwards communications—that filter the important signals from the ground from the background noise—can reap dividends and inform longer-term planning" (CIPD, 2011). From an organizational design perspective, the focus of organization development is based upon the beginning, being purpose and the reason for an organizations existence, whereas traditional change management methodologies appear to focus on the design and science of structure and seemingly forget the behavioral element when formulating strategy.

Turning the design components of an organization on its head, as per the organizational balance model, rather than designing an organization around what strategic goals and task structure release the human element of the organization rather than controls and suppresses these elements within the organization. Organization development provides the tools and techniques required to diagnose human process issues and interventions to come before focusing on strategic management processes, technostructural, and technology design issues. In managing change within the organization, it must always be understood that it is people who need to change first and foremost. If you cannot change the people that the change is affecting, regardless of the fabulous technology, structure, or processes that you introduce, will struggle to become embedded. Focusing on the human elements within the organization is the key. Measuring behavioral outcomes as suggested by OD practitioners are certainly a very good start point. Understanding how these outcomes impact and are aligned to organizational purpose are key when reviewing organizational balance, and using OD tools to design interventions that are in congruence or in harmony with the organizational purpose will support organizational cycling.

The key to finding balance is for an organization to fully understanding the full impact of balance throughout its operations now and in the future. An organizations leadership must be mindful of what elements are within the organization, which can be disrupted or help achieve balance. Some of the biggest impacts on an organization's balance when you have assessed the organizations life cycle may be areas that you have not considered. For example, Bruno Berthon (2008) explained that "when Cadbury performed a life-cycle assessment on its Dairy Milk bar, the company discovered that the biggest environmental impact came from the methane generated by cows producing the milk rather than from the transportation, packaging or processing of the finished product."

Organizational Cycling

Organizational cycling therefore is the process of receiving inputs from the environment and supporting the continuous process of change and transformation that must combine all the elements of organizational balance to move the organization toward balance before the next disruptive force comes along. Its main focus is on a process of continuous change but with the focus being on designing for performance through the human element, led by the organization's leaders and releasing the Talent Within. In this way, organizational cycling is outside of the organizational balance model but holds each element in tension in response to external forces and disruption to keep the organization moving. On the one hand, it is symbiotic with the external environment; on the other hand, it keeps the organization moving forward so the disruption adds to the energy without knocking the organization off course. Metaphorically, organizational cycling is like the car that individuals travel in. It is the vehicle that is in motion that takes the driver left or right to avoid obstacles and, where necessary, provides protection from the outside forces while providing the mechanism with which the individual can avoid collision with outside forces. In this way, it carries the organization rather than becoming part of the organization, forever in motion, forever moving forward. If the organization fails to take notice of the input from the external environment, failing to make the necessary adjustments and changes, then a collision will happen. In this way, although organizational cycling is part of the other elements of organizational balance, the other elements of the organizational balance model are not part of organizational cycling.

Summary

- There are many influences on organizational balance, forces that can cause disruption, lessons that can be learned, and the inversion of organizational development and design processes.
- The dynamism of the business environment means balance must be fought for in seemingly endless streams of competing demands requiring rebalancing.
- Change management traditionally focuses on the technostructural factors of an organization's design.
- The key to finding balance is for an organization to fully understand the full impact of balance throughout its operations now and in the future.
- Organizational cycling therefore is the process of receiving inputs from the environment and supporting the continuous process of change and transformation.
- Organizational Development practice provides tools that can be utilized to rebalance the organization in line with the organizational context.
- Although organizational cycling is part of the other elements of organizational balance, the other elements of the organizational balance model are not part of organizational cycling.

Conclusions

From the perspective of achieving organizational balance, all the elements of an organization's performance need to operate together in the same way as an ecosystem. Organizations need to change because society has changed and hierarchical technostructural approaches to organization design are no longer fully fit for purpose in today's fast-moving, knowledge-intensive world. Organizations operating in the modern global economy need to adapt their traditional thinking of how they operate to a philosophy that embraces the natural cycles, systems, controls, and available talent within the organization in order to achieve balance and create an environment for sustainable performance. This is where the Organization Balance model seeks to offer an alternative approach to organization design.

The model of organizational balance provides a framework of interrelationships and interactions that are specific to the human processes within the organization, which have an impact on the sustainable organizational performance. Taking into account the holistic nature of an organization, each section of the framework describes a human process element of the organizational ecosystem, which interacts with other elements and results in a positive or negative impact on organizational performance.

The world has moved on from the industrial revolution concept of human endeavor. Human beings are not machines; if they are to perform in a sustainable way they cannot be standardized and put into boxes. If their potential is to be released and an environment for sustainable performance is to be created, humans cannot be treated as machines— They think, they feel, they are individual. Organizational Balance can be achieved when the human elements within the organization are supported and encouraged to flourish with the organizational environment alongside the physical structures, processes, and systems.

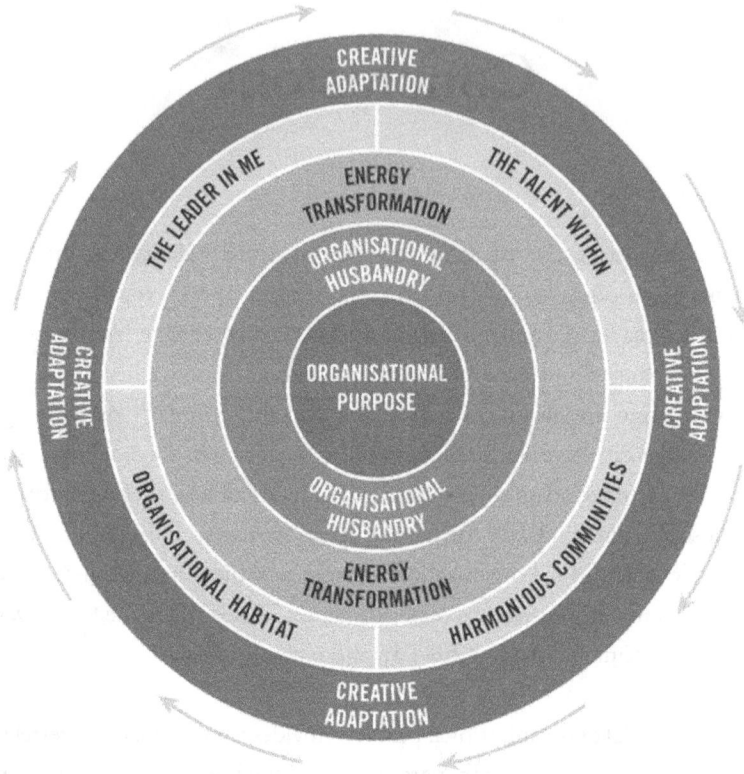

Model of organizational balance

Organizational Purpose

As the human heart, organization's purpose is more than just the center of organization, it provides the lifeblood to the whole of the organizational system. It connects, refreshes, renews, and brings life to every single corner of the organization. If any part of the organization becomes disconnected from the purpose of the organization, it will wither and fail to function properly, like a limb cut from the body's blood supply.

The Leader in Me

The leadership team should be made up of both leaders of people and leaders of expertise. Without both types of leader in the leadership team, organizational balance will not be possible. Too much emphasis on people will mean that competitive advantage from expert knowledge will remain unharnessed; too much emphasis on expertise and the engagement of the workforce will suffer. Either scenario is equally catastrophic for the creation of sustainable performance.

The Talent Within

Part of identifying talent is for individuals to build self-awareness around what they just do and to begin a self-appreciation of the talent of doing things that come naturally and easily to them. In addition conversations with their colleagues about what their colleague's value in them will also highlight areas of talent. Once talent has been identified, it is important that both the organization and the individual invest resource (time and money) to develop the talent within.

Harmonious Communities

By tapping into the collective talent gathered from around the networked organization, it is possible to use group cohesion cross-functionally to complete business-related tasks. If employees are able to collaborate in the truest sense, the community as a whole responds to a needs-based process, they may not simply do what they are told, but are able to form cohesive groups that think differently about what is needed to help achieve the organization's purpose. Relationship building is an essential element of this process, and time must be given to ensure quality relationships can be developed.

Organizational Habitat

The networked structure will also allow the organization to achieve synergy and leverage the talent within when and where is required in a timely manner, enabling the organization to exploit possible opportunities when they occur. From an individual employee's perspective, the networked structure will increase the opportunity for individuals to build and develop their strengths and competencies, increase expertise, and release the potential of talent within the organization as a whole.

Organization Husbandry

Organization husbandry has to be seen in a holistic framework and solutions cannot be taken in isolation. Understanding the wider system within which the solution is operating can help those making the decision be aware of possible unintended consequences a decision made today may have on future generations. Organizations must have responsibility for and demonstrate a commitment to environmental stewardship and citizenship. Organizations also have a responsibility to help individuals to release their talent potential and use their talent. Waste of talent is similar to the misuse of a natural asset, foolishly wasting nonreplaceable natural assets or the plundering of natural resources that should be saved for future generations; such a waste is surely intolerable.

Creative Adaptation

Innovation and creativity require space and time for people to cogitate. This means, of course, that innovation is a way of life. People throughout the organization need to be empowered to spend time thinking about the various problems that might occur, so when the problem does occur there is already an answer ready to go, or, at the very least, a number of options that can be worked on to develop further.

Energy Transformation

Energy transformation is a determination by the organization that, regardless of the input, the transformation process will lead to outcomes that will disrupt the world in a positive way. This will be not only through sustainable practices as discussed in organizational husbandry but also in individual, group, and organizational interventions, which in and of themselves are deliberately positive. This means for every action there needs to be an awareness of the reaction to that action. There is thoughtfulness in energy transformation that demands a responsibility and accountability for outcomes.

Organizational Cycling

Organizational cycling is the process of receiving inputs from the environment and supporting the continuous process of change and transformation that must combine all the elements of organizational balance to move the organization toward balance before the next disruptive force comes along. Its focus is on a process of continuous change, but with the focus being on designing for performance through the human element, led by the organization's leaders and releasing the Talent Within. In this way, organizational cycling is outside of the organizational balance model but holds each element in tension in response to external forces and disruption to keep the organization moving.

This framework of interrelationships and interactions is specific to the human processes within the organization, which, from an organizational design perspective, have a significant impact on organizational performance. Taking into account the holistic nature of an organization, each section of the framework describes a human process element of the organizational ecosystem, which interacts with other elements and results in a positive or negative impact on organizational performance. The organization balance model offers an approach to organization design in business, which is humanistic. It seeks to work with the human organizational system, overcoming resistance, drag, and natural barriers to deliver success and positively affect the organization's performance. Working within the organizational system, the organization balance model designs for performance that is self-sustaining and seeks to help organizational leaders to develop a deep understanding of the balance of the organization.

References

Argyris, C., and D.A. Schon. 1996. *Organiational learning II*. Boston, MA: Addison Wesley.

Beswick, C. 2011. "Seven Steps to Innovation." *Training Journal*, pp. 21–25.

Blair, T. 2010. *A Journey*. London, UK: Hutchinson.

Brewerton, P. 2011. "The Power of the Team." *Training Journal*, pp. 37–40.

Berthon, B.J.G. 2008. Achieving Performance: *The Sustainability Imperative*. Dublin, Republic of Ireland: Accenture.

Buckingham, M.A. 1999. *First Break All the Rules—What the World's Greatest Managers Do Differently*. Washington, D.C: The Gallup Organization.

Chambers, E.G., M. Foulon, H. Handfield-Jones, S.M. Hankin, and E.G. Michaels. 1998. "The War for Talent." *McKinsey Quarterly*, pp. 44–57.

CIPD. 2011. *Shaping the Future—Sustainable Organizational Performance: What Really Makes the Difference*. London, UK: CIPD.

CIPD. 2010. *Shared Purpose: The Golden Thread*. London, UK: CIPD.

CIPD. 2003. *Understanding the People and Performance Link: Unlocking the Black Box*. London, UK: CIPD.

Cummings, T.G. 2009. *Organization Development and Change*. Boston, MA: South Western CENGAGE Learning.

Curtis, C. 2011. Head of Talent Performance and Leadership Development Santander.

Eveleth, R. 2013. Computer Programming Used to Be Women's Work. *Smithsonian Magazine*.

Eyre, E. 2011a. "70/20/10 Model Represents a New Focus for L&D." *Training Journal*, pp. 10–12.

Eyre, E. 2011b. "Lack of Honest Feedback on Performance Endangers Staff Motivation." *Training Journal*, p. 9.

Eyre, E. 2011c. "Survey Reveals Lack of Leadership Skills to Cope with Convergence." *Training Journal*, pp. 12–13.

Foster, C., N. Moore, and P. Stokes. 2014. *Rethinking Talent Management in Organizations: Towards a Boundary-less Model* (The paper appears as Chapter Two in the academic book). In *Innovative Business Practices: Prevailing a Turbulent Era, eds.* D. Vrontis, and A. Thrassou. Cambridge, UK: Cambridge Scholars Publishing.

Foster, C. 2015. "Managing the Flow of Talent through Organisations—A Boundary-less Model." *Development and Learning in Organizations* 29, no. 1, pp. 15–19.

Foster, C. 2017a. *Designing Learning and Development for Return on Investment.* Singapore: Business Expert Press.

Foster, C. 2017b. *Talent Management.* Singapore: Expert Insights, Business Expert Press.

Foster, C. 2017c. *The HR Practitioner.* Singapore: Expert Insights, Business Expert Press.

Foster, C. 2017d. *Developing Agile Leaders.* Singapore: Expert Insights, Business Expert Press.

Future Foundation. 2010. The Decisive Decade: The Acceleration of Ideas Will Transform the Workplace by 2020. Google http://lp.google-mkto.com/rs/google/images/Google-Decisive-Decade-Report-Future-Foundation.pdf, (accessed August 23, 2017).

Gladwell, M. 2002. "The Talent Myth." *The New Yorker* 22, pp. 28–33.

Hoey, J. 2011. "Using the Past to Try to Predict the Future." *Training Journal*, pp. 43–46.

John Lewis, P. 2010. *Annual Report and Accounts* 2010. London, UK: John Lewis Partnership.

Kates, A. and Galbraith, J.R. 2007. *Designing Your Organization. Using the Star Model to Solve 5 Critical Design Challenges.* San Francisco, CA: Jossey-Bass.

Katz, N., D. Lazer, H. Arrow, and N. Contractor. 2004. Network theory and small groups. *Small Group Research* 35, no. 3, pp. 307–332.

Katzenbach, J.R., and D.K. Smith. 1993. *The Discipline of Teams.* Boston, MA: Harvard Business Press.

Lawler III, E.E. 2008. *Talent: Making People Your Competitive Advantage.* Hoboken, NJ: Jossey-Bass.

Lee, G. 2007. *Leadership Coaching from Personal Insight to Organizational Performance*. London, UK: Chartered Institute of Personnel and Development.

Maslow, A.H. 1943. "A Theory of Human Motivation." *Psychological Review* 50, no. 4, p.370.

Maslow, A.H., R. Frager, and J. Fadiman. 1970. *Motivation and Personality* (Vol. 2, pp. 1887–1904). New York, NY: Harper & Row.

Mayer, D. 2007. "Corporate Citizenship and Trustworthy Capitalism: Cocreating a More Peaceful Planet." *American Business Law Journal* 44, no. 2, pp. 237–286.

McGurk, J. January, 2011. Working Together for Success. *People Management*, p. 36.

Milligan, A. 2002. *Uncommon Practice People Who Deliver Great Brand Experience*. Harlow, UK: Pearson Education Limited.

Peter, L.J., and R. Hull. 1969. *The Peter Principle* (No. 04; RMD, PN6231. M2 P4). London, UK: Souvenir Press.

Reis, E., 2009. *Minimum Viable Product: A Guide*. Startup Lessons Learned.

Roe, A. 2011. Director Barclay Meade. Interview.

Russ-Eft, D.F. 2014. "Human Resource Development, Evaluation, and Sustainability: What are the Relationships?" *Human Resource Development International* 17, no. 5, pp. 545–559.

Russ, S.W., and C.E. Wallace. Fall, 2013. "Pretend Play and Creative Processes." *American Journal of Play* 6, no. 1, pp. 136–148.

Stuart-Kotze, R. 2008. *Who Are Your Best People*. Great Britain, UK: Pearson Education Limited.

Warren, R. 2002. *The Purpose Driven Life; What an Earth Am I Here for?* Grand Rapids, Michigan: Zondervan.

Wickens, P.D. 1995. *The Ascendant Organisation*. London, UK: MacMillan.

Yeung, R. 2010. *The Extra One Per cent—How Small Changes Make Exceptional People*. London, UK: Macmillan.

Index

OTHER TITLES IN THE HUMAN RESOURCE MANAGEMENT AND ORGANIZATIONAL BEHAVIOR COLLECTION

- *Power Quotes: For Life, Business, and Leadership* by Danai Krokou
- *Magnificent Leadership: Transform Uncertainty, Transcend Circumstance, Claim the Future* by Sarah Levitt
- *Negotiating with Winning Words: Dialogue and Skills to Help You Come Out Ahead in Any Business Negotiation* by Michael Schatzki
- *Conflict First Aid: How to Stop Personality Clashes and Disputes from Damaging You or Your Organization* by Nancy Radford
- *Temperatism, Volume I: A New Way to Think About Business and Doing Good* by Carrie Foster
- *The Challenge to Be and Not to Do: How to Manage Your Career and Maximize Your Potential* by Carrie Foster
- *Slow Down to Speed Up: Lead, Succeed, and Thrive in a 24/7 World* by Liz Bywater
- *The Illusion of Inclusion: Global Inclusion, Unconscious Bias, and the Bottom Line* by Helen Turnbull
- *On All Cylinders: The Entrepreneur's Handbook* by Ron Robinson
- *Employee LEAPS: Leveraging Engagement by Applying Positive Strategies* by Kevin E. Phillips
- *Making Human Resource Technology Decisions: A Strategic Perspective* by Janet H. Marler and Sandra L. Fisher
- *Feet to the Fire: How to Exemplify And Create The Accountability That CreatesGreat Companies* by Lorraine A. Moore
- *HR Analytics and Innovations in Workforce Planning* by Tony Miller
- *Deconstructing Management Maxims, Volume I: A Critical Examination of Conventional Business Wisdom* by Kevin Wayne
- *Deconstructing Management Maxims, Volume II: A Critical Examination of Conventional Business Wisdom* by Kevin Wayne
- *The Real Me: Find and Express Your Authentic Self* by Mark Eyre
- *Across the Spectrum: What Color Are You?* by Stephen Elkins-Jarrett

Announcing the Business Expert Press Digital Library

Concise e-books business students need for classroom and research

This book can also be purchased in an e-book collection by your library as

- *a one-time purchase,*
- *that is owned forever,*
- *allows for simultaneous readers,*
- *has no restrictions on printing, and*
- *can be downloaded as PDFs from within the library community.*

Our digital library collections are a great solution to beat the rising cost of textbooks. E-books can be loaded into their course management systems or onto students' e-book readers. The **Business Expert Press** digital libraries are very affordable, with no obligation to buy in future years. For more information, please visit **www.businessexpertpress.com/librarians**. To set up a trial in the United States, please email **sales@businessexpertpress.com**.

www.ingramcontent.com/pod-product-compliance
Lightning Source LLC
Chambersburg PA
CBHW071837200326
41519CB00016B/4143